INTRODUCTION TO SQL SERVER

BASIC SKILLS FOR ANY SQL SERVER USER

Bert Scalzo, PhD.

K. Brian Kelley, MVP - SQL Server

DEDICATION

To my past and present miniature schnauzers Ziggy and Max -
the two most wonderful four-legged kids that any parent could
ever have :

And to my wife Susan who's always jealous of my many book
dedications solely to the dogs...

Bert Scalzo, PhD.

INTRODUCTION TO SQL SERVER

BASIC SKILLS FOR ANY SQL SERVER USER

Bert Scalzo, PhD.

K. Brian Kelley, MVP - SQL Server

Copyright © 2011 by **Texas Publishing**.

ISBN: 1451504632

EAN-13:   9781451504637

CONTENTS

CHAPTER 10: DATABASE SANDBOX 141

AUTHOR BIO'S 151

ACKNOWLEDGEMENTS

I've been doing database work, including data modeling, for more than two decades. Much of what I've learned has come from other great people who were very willing to share their expertise and/or knowledge with me. So rather than list a few people and risk missing anyone, let me just say thanks to all those people *"along the way"* who've helped me to learn so much. I could not have gotten to where I am without them.

Bert Scalzo, PhD.

A special thanks to Bert Scalzo for giving me the opportunity to do this book project with him. Thanks also goes to Kevin E. Kline for putting the two of us together for the book. Finally, thanks to my family, who are always a foundation for me.

K. Brian Kelley, MVP - SQL Server

PREFACE

These days everything is more or less computerized, with self service via applications and the web making us all regular, mass consumers of data. Thus unlike days past where databases and those who worked with them were considered a specialty, now database access and work is now deemed quite common - in fact so much so that databases are simply regarded as a commodity. Hence more and more people, both technical and not, find themselves needing to access and work with data in SQL Server databases.

This book is meant for specifically that audience - those people new to SQL Server who either know the business or have some technical skills, and all of whom now find themselves thrust into the world of accessing and working with data in a SQL Server database. This book seeks to collect all the basic or fundamental skills and knowledge necessary into one easy to read yet valuable reference book. Our goal is simply to have this one book assist everyone to be successful with SQL Server.

CHAPTER 1: TERMINOLOGY

To begin working with a "SQL Server Database", we first must define what the words "SQL Server" and "Database" actually mean. Then we will build upon that most basic vocabulary to add additional terms you're likely to hear - such as "schema", "table", and "index".

DEFINITION OF DATA

Data is an asset - in fact it's any company's most valuable asset. You cannot effectively perform your business functions without the ability to comprehend and process that data. In reality much of what people typically think of as "work experience" is nothing more than knowledge of business data and processes.

DEFINITION OF DATABASE

In business terms, a database is quite simply a warehouse or repository of your business' data. For example the company's customer and order information might constitute what it considers as its data or database. Another way to think of this is that the business data or database is nothing more than a snapshot of what your "data at rest" appears like (i.e. not in flux or being processed). Thus it is the non-technical means by which the business both recognizes and comprehends its data.

In technical terms, database simply refers to the highly specialized computer software utilized to house, manage and access that business data. Some examples of database software include Oracle, IBM DB2, Microsoft SQL Server and MySQL. These are simply tools for getting at your data. It's the data itself that is the item or asset of value. Databases such as SQL Server are nothing than tools to work with that asset.

Where most confusion enters is that people will often equate the business concept with the technology used to implement it. It does not matter whether business' data assets are housed in simple files or database software, the business has a repository or database of data it needs to function. But many people will assume that when you say database that you mean the data assets are housed within such database software. Therefore the word "database" has almost universally become synonymous with the tools' technology.

As such, you will often hear your companies' business databases referred to as something like the following: Our mission critical SQL Server database for customers and their orders. But the truth is that the word SQL Server is the least important part of that statement. Because the business could later re-implement that database in another database software technology - and then the data asset reference might instead read: Our mission critical Oracle database for customers and their orders. So don't let the software tool itself become the center of the universe. Remember that the software is simply how the business concept has been implemented at this point in time.

RELATIONAL DATABASES

So what then is a "relational" database? As you work with more technical people in your company, you are sure to hear this word. It is nothing magical, simply meaning that the database software organizes, accesses and presents your data as "tables". Think of a database table like a worksheet in Microsoft Excel, it has rows and columns. Sometimes you'll hear the rows referred to as records. That's it.

The reason that relational databases became so important is that they were the very first and only database software whose approach was more logical rather than physical. Older database technologies (e.g. hierarchical and network databases) were more technically or programmer oriented. That is to say that rows or records in one table pointed to any related rows in the same or different tables via a physical pointer - such as a file or disk drive address, as shown here in Figure 1.

EMPLOYEE		
Name	**Job**	**Department Pointer**
John Smith	Clerk	X000FFFEE
Jane Doe	Clerk	X000FFFEE
Bill Becker	Manager	X000FFFEE
Joe Haskins	Clerk	X000FFFAA
Mary Mavis	Manager	X000FFFAA

Figure 1: Non-Relational Table

So in order to access the employees who work in the "Accounting" department, the database user would have to find that row in the department table and note its address, then retrieve the employee rows that pointed to that very same physical address for their department.

Whereas in relational databases all the row connections are performed via more logical values, namely human readable ones. Thus the very same employee table as a relational construct would be much easier to read as shown here in Figure 2.

EMPLOYEE		
Name	Job	Department
John Smith	Clerk	Accounting
Jane Doe	Clerk	Accounting
Bill Becker	Manager	Accounting
Joe Haskins	Clerk	Shipping
Mary Mavis	Manager	Shipping

Figure 2: Relational Table

So in order to access the employees who work in the "Accounting" department one just needs to search based upon that very simple yet business meaningful reference. That's the beauty of the relational model: it separates the internal physical storage and connectivity aspects totally away from the user access approach.

In fact Edgar Codd (who pioneered relational database theory in the early 1970's) devised 12 key rules as to what constitutes relational database management systems. Of those 12 rules, we have now covered the first two most fundamental and highly critical rules:

- **The Information rule:** All information in a relational database is represented logically in just one way - namely by values in column positions within rows of tables.

- **The Guaranteed Access rule:** Each item of data in a relational database is guaranteed to be logically accessible by resorting to a combination of table name, primary key value, and column name.

It's this second rule that we need investigate and understand better - as it introduces the concept of keys.

PRIMARY KEYS

The primary key is defined as the column or combination of column values in a table that represent a unique or singular method for identifying or separating one business entity or concept from another. So if we're talking about customers it might be something as simple as a customer number, whereas for an order it might be the combination of the customer number making the order and the date of that order.

Note that the primary key is a business concept and its associated database rule, and not the internal mechanism used to enforce or guarantee that result. For that, the database needs indexes - which are nothing more than a tool for speeding up access to rows of data based upon their logical value and which can also be utilized to enforce or guarantee their uniqueness.

Let's look at the common phone book as an example. The primary key or business rule might be that no two persons can have the same phone number - thus the combination of the phone number and the person's name must be unique. As we scan the phone book we sort of just accept that fact - that is we don't need anything special to signify it. But now as we scan the phone book to quickly find a particular person's phone number, we use the index values on the top of the page - as we know that the peoples' names are ordered in alphabetical order and will fall between the top left and top right most listed index values.

So in database terms, we therefore have a primary key that says the combination of the person name and phone number is unique - and internally requires an index to ensure it. Plus we might need an index for fast access on just the name. So the constraint and its internal index are to enforce a business rule or requirement, whereas an index by itself is merely a tool to speed up access to rows of data. This difference is critical - and one that generally confuses very many people using relational databases.

So in short here are the main differences between a primary key and an index:

- **Primary Key**

    ❑ Business rule or Requirement

    ❑ Always Unique

    ❑ Permanent Fixture (Always On)

    ❑ Requires an Index to Enforce

- **Index**

    ❑ Used to Speed Up Data Access

    ❑ Dynamic In Nature (i.e. can be Added & Dropped as Needed)

    ❑ Unique or Non-Unique

FOREIGN KEYS

The concept of a foreign key is tightly related to relational rule #2 - the guaranteed access rule. It's also one of the most important and useful mechanisms for relating data - hence the name relational database. As shown here in Figure 3, the "child table" (i.e. employee) rows point logically to the associated "parent table" (i.e. department) rows via the foreign key column - which is simply the parent table's primary key column(s) copied as a logical pointer or reference column into the child table.

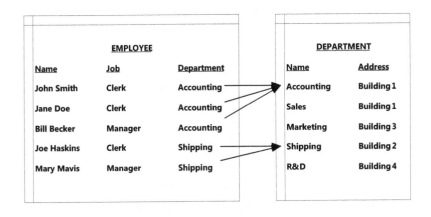

Figure 3: Foreign Key

This foreign key construct enables us to "join" the parent and child tables (which will be more thoroughly explained in the later chapter on Structured Query Language or SQL). In essence this means that we can logically combine the parent and child data rows that are related as if that data was all just in one big row. So if we wanted a report showing the name, job and address for each employee - we could construct that by doing a join between employee and department and using the combined rows to obtain our required report values.

As with the primary key, a foreign key is a business concept and its associated database rule too, and not the internal mechanism used to enforce or guarantee that result. Once again indexes, in this case non-unique, are needed to both effectively and efficiently maintain these parent and child table data relationships. In fact for many database management systems the lack of a foreign key index can slow down the queries as you would expect - but also all operations on the parent and child tables due to complex row locking strategies required for the internal database processing.

It's worth noting that some databases don't offer foreign keys, and many applications built on top of relational databases that do lack foreign keys due to poor design. Since foreign keys simply implement business rules that you already know and live by, they are simply a mechanism to enforce what's supposed to be true. If they are missing, it might be time to see about adding them.

SCHEMAS AND USERS

Not all database management systems have the basic concept of a schema. SQL Server does, but how schemas are implemented differ between versions of SQL Server up to SQL Server 2000 and versions from SQL Server 2005 on. In both cases, schemas represent a means of grouping database objects. In SQL Server 2000 and prior, a schema is simply a database user account and all of the database objects owned by that user. In SQL Server 2005 and above, a schema represents a container for grouping objects and the schema is owned by a single database user. However, unlike previous versions of SQL Server, a database user can own multiple schemas.

In versions up to SQL Server 2000, some database users own database objects such as tables and stored procedure, whereas others simply have the ability to connect to the database and then to look at other people database objects (if they've been granted access). In SQL Server 2005 and above, it's common to see schemas owned by database users, but it's not very common for users to own individual objects. While that's still possible in rare cases where particular security measures have to be implemented, typically objects inherit ownership from the schemas which contain them.

You may hear the terms database schema and user utilized interchangeably. It's not uncommon to say schema when talking about object ownership and user when talking about connecting to the database (as in user id or user name), even when talking about newer versions of SQL Server.

DATABASE NAME

Every SQL Server database has a unique name by which users reference it. Think of this name like a phone number for the database, it's the reference name way by which you refer to or call it. You need to obtain this database name from your DBA as you'll need it for most real world work you'll attempt to perform.

SERVER INSTANCE

Each installation of SQL Server is known as an instance of SQL Server. Starting with SQL Server 2000, it is possible to have multiple installations, and therefore multiple instances of SQL Server, on the same computer. Each instance of SQL Server will have multiple databases.

Therefore, in order to access the data contained within SQL Server, not only do you need to know the database name, but you also need to know the server instance. In some cases this will simply be the name of the computer, such as MySQLServer, but it could also be what we call a named instance, such as MySQLServer\OrderingServer.

CONCLUSION

In this chapter we reviewed the basic SQL Server vocabulary that one should possess in order to understand how to work with their SQL Server databases. Once you comprehend and appreciate terms such as data, database, table, primary keys, foreign keys, indexes, schemas, database names and server instances, you have all the requisites to work with most any SQL Server database. Thus armed with this information you should never again feel like you're hearing worthless "gobbledygook" during any conversation about your SQL Server database. You'll be in the know.

CHAPTER 2: PREPARATION

To successfully connect to and work with a SQL Server Database from your Windows PC (desktop or notebook), there are several things that must be properly setup or configured. None of these are very complex, but failure to address these items can and will result in either problems, warnings and/or errors. So while this chapter may be brief, the basic concepts (and their mental images) are nonetheless very critical for your success. So it would be wise to read and learn this chapter's material well.

DATABASE ARCHITECTURE

The SQL Server database itself will most often reside upon a server somewhere within your organization. While you can both run and access the SQL Server database on most PC's these days, the raw performance, tight security and high availability requirements alone generally require a secure, centrally managed database server. Hence for most people your SQL Server database will be on a server and have the 50,000 foot overall or high level architecture like that shown here in Figure 1.

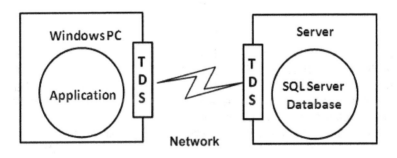

Figure 1: Database Architecture

The critical item of note is that both the client and the server need some supporting SQL Server network library files in order for communication between your application and the database to occur. The TDS you see in Figure 1 refers to the protocol, or how an application and SQL Server talk to each other. Because it's not necessary to know anything about TDS to connect to a SQL Server database, we won't delve any further into the specifics about it.

What is important is you must have those network library files on your PC for database connections to function properly. Since Windows 2000, all versions of Windows have at least a basic set of these network library files already pre-installed. SQL Server 2005 introduced a new set of network files called the SQL Server Native Client which provides additional functionality based on new features that was added to that version of SQL Server. The features are not essential to retrieve data from a SQL Server database but center around security and management functionality such as the ability to handle passwords similar to the way Windows does. However, if you don't use these additional features, chances are you already have everything you need to connect to the SQL Server database.

DATABASE VERSIONS

The SQL Server database, like most software, has different versions – such as SQL Server 2000, 2005, 2008, and 2008 R2. These are simply the marketing names for the initial or base releases. In addition there are numerous patches available, usually called service packs or cumulative updates. If you're experiencing an issue with something not working the way you'd expect it to, you might check with your system administrator or database administrator to see if one of these is needed. But typically they are only required if you installed specific client software from the SQL Server CDs/DVDs.

CONNECTING

Thus far we've primarily covered terminology and that is a prerequisite for successfully working with your SQL Server databases. Now it's time to perform your very first SQL Server database task – connecting to your database. That may seem like an anticlimactic task but it's the first step in making use of the data within those databases.

Think of creating the database connection like making a phone call. If you don't have the proper equipment, a service plan, the number of whom you're calling and knowledge of how to dial that number, then you cannot initiate a phone call and thus cannot hold a meaningful conversation. The same is true for databases. You must successfully connect before you can retrieve, insert or update your data.

CONNECTING VIA ODBC

A lot of applications connect to SQL Server using a method called ODBC. Either the application will present an interface where you can create your connection or it will ask you for an existing ODBC connection. Chances are that if it presents an interface, the steps will be similar to when you create your own ODBC connection. In fact, a lot of times applications will simply re-use Windows' own tool for managing these connections. So let's look at how to do that.

In order to find the tool which creates ODBC connections, go to your Start button, and you should see an icon for your Control Panel, like in Figure 2.

Figure 2: Control Panel icon

You'll want to click on it and that will bring up the Control Panel. If you're in Classic View, you should see an icon for **Administrative Tools**. If you're in Category View you'll have to double-click on the **Performance and Maintenance icon** first. Once you see the **Administrative Tools** icon, double-click on it and you should have a new list of options. What you're looking for is the icon for **Data Sources (ODBC)**. Double-click on it and it will bring up the tool ODBC Administrator where you'll be able to configure a new ODBC connection.

When you first launch the ODBC Administrator you will see the main screen as shown in Figure Figure 3 – don't be surprised if there are no predefined ODBC data sources. There are two types of data sources called data set names (i.e. DSN): user and system. User ones can only be seen and used by the current Windows user, whereas system ones can be seen and used by any Windows user on that same PC.

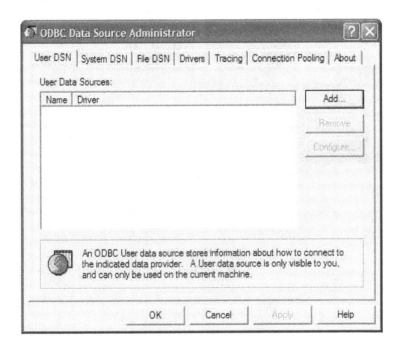

Figure 3: ODBC Admin Main Screen

When you press the "*Add*" button, you will see the wizard's first page as shown here in Figure 4 – where you are to pick the method to connect to the data. Here we have a good number of choices, but usually you'll just want the one that says SQL Server. In this example, the full SQL Server tools are installed for several versions of SQL Server, which is why you also see choices for SQL Server Native Client. You likely won't have the SQL Server Native

Client choices unless you need them. Simply select SQL Server and click Finish.

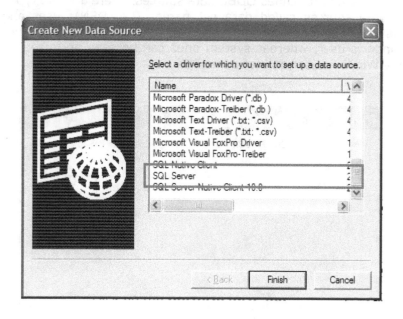

Figure 4: SQL Server Data Source

In the event that you'll one day need to connect to a different database server (Oracle, DB2, etc.) generally speaking you will have the most reliable results and fastest performance using the ODBC driver from the database vendor and it likely will be named so you easily recognize it.

Once you've chosen your ODBC driver, you then need to assign some properties to this new data source as shown here in Figure 5 – with the two most important being the data source name (i.e. what your application will refer to as the connection) and the name of the SQL Server you are connecting to.

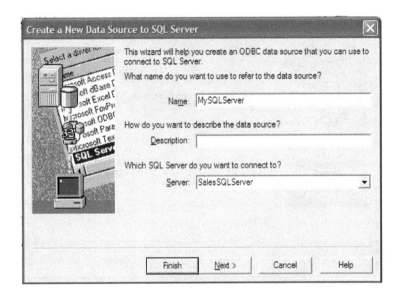

Figure 5: Choose the Name and SQL Server

In Figure 5 I am naming my connection MySQLServer and I'm connecting to a SQL Server named SalesSQLServer. If you are unsure of the name for the server, check with your system or database administrator.

You'll then need to choose *how* you connect to the SQL Server in the sense of how does SQL Server know who you are. Most of the time, you'll connect using the user account you logged on to Windows with. If you need a special SQL Server login, your system or database administrator should provide it ahead of time, along with the appropriate password. In either case, make the appropriate selections for the next screen, shown in Figure 6. If you're to use your Windows user account, leave the option set to use Windows NT authentication. That's the default.

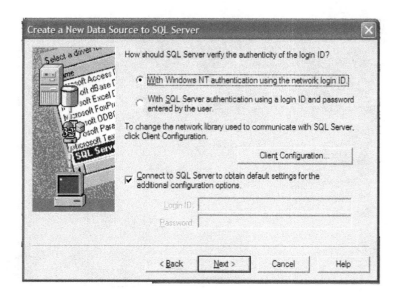

Figure 6: Tell SQL Server Who You Are

Next, you'll need to specify any other options for the connection. In Figure 7, you'll see an option to specify the database. Here you'll want to check the checkbox to change the default database and then choose the right one from the drop down list. If you should get an error here, it means either the SQL Server you specified in the previous screen is not available, or you mistyped its name, or you don't have permission to connect. If that's the case, go back to the previous screen, check the name of the SQL Server, and if you believe its right, follow up with your system or database administrator. It could be down or there could be another reason as to why you can't connect to it.

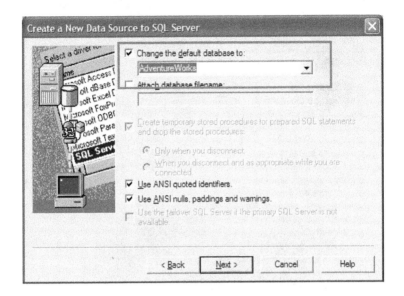

Figure 7: Specify the Database

In Figure 7 I'm specifying the database AdventureWorks. This is the database I know contains the sales information I want to access. You'll need to know both the server and the database name to get at the data stored on the SQL Server.

Click the Next button to go to the last configuration screen, where you likely won't need to make any changes, then click Finish to create your ODBC connection. You should be presented with a screen like in - be sure to test your connection to make sure everything is fine before clicking OK.

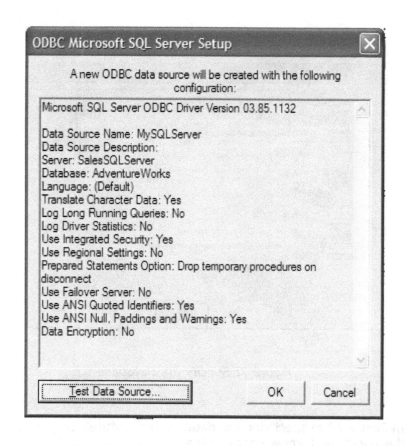

Figure 8: Review Setup

CONCLUSION

In this chapter we reviewed the basic concepts and processes you need to understand and perform in order to begin successfully working with your SQL Server databases. We also reviewed covered the prerequisite knowledge to tackle the first and most critical database task – connecting. Much like a phone call – we entered the information necessary to dial in to the database and then placed the call.

CHAPTER 3: SQL SERVER MANAGEMENT STUDIO

The standard tool used by database administrators and database developers is SQL Server Management Studio (SSMS). It's a client tool that comes with SQL Server and can be installed on any Windows operating system from Windows XP SP3 and up.

STARTING UP SSMS

If you have the SQL Server media, you can choose to install just the client tools to your workstation. Once you've done that, depending on the version of SQL Server client tools you have installed (2005 vs. 2008) you should find SSMS either under the SQL Server 2005 or SQL Server 2008 folder from the Start menu. Figure 1 shows its location for SQL Server 2005. It is possible and acceptable to have the tools installed both for versions.

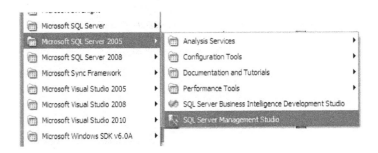

Figure 1: SSMS Location

When you first start up SSMS, by default it will bring up the connection dialog window (Figure 2). This allows you to connect to a SQL Server right away.

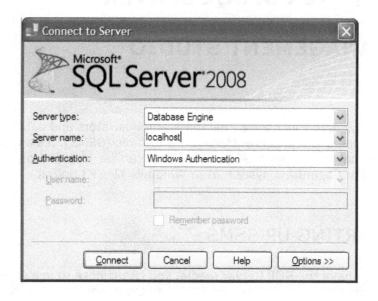

Figure 2: Connection Dialog Window

If you don't want to connect to one immediately, or you aren't sure which one to connect to, you can simply cancel out. SSMS gives an option to have a list of registered servers that you can refer to at any time, but we'll look at that shortly.

OBJECT EXPLORER

If you've chosen to connect to a SQL Server, the connection will be displayed in the left pane of SSMS in a window called Object Explorer. Here you can take a look at the SQL Server in question and navigate through the database, the database objects, the security, etc., depending on your rights and permissions on the given SQL Server. The Object Explorer is shown in figure 3.

Figure 3: Object Explorer

Don't worry if your Object Explorer doesn't have all the same icons mine does or if your menu bar doesn't have all the same menu items as the ones in the figures. SSMS allows for something called add-ins which can extend the functionality of SQL Server Management Studio and I have several installed, which explains the differences. We'll talk about add-ins in a later section and I'll recommend a very useful one to grab which is completely free.

REGISTERED SERVERS

I mentioned that you could register servers with SSMS and then you wouldn't have to necessarily remember the name of the SQL Server when you first start up SSMS. In the same window as Object Explorer, there should be a tab at the bottom which reads Registered Servers. If it's not there, you can make it visible by going to View > Registered Servers. Figure 4 shows a list of several registered servers.

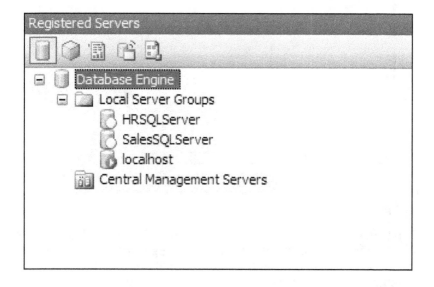

Figure 4: Registered Servers

To register a server, you'll need to know the SQL Server name and how you're supposed to connect to it (see chapter 2 if you are uncertain how to do this). You can create folders to group your registered server, but the default groups are Local Server Groups and (if you are SSMS 2008) Central Management Servers. Right-click on the folder where you want to put the registered server and choose New Server Registration (Figure 5).

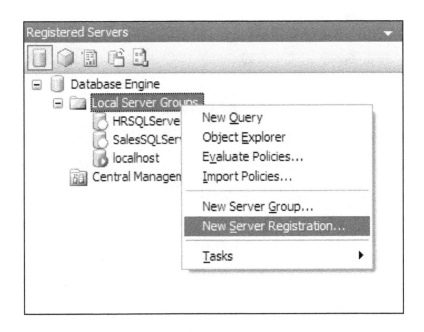

Figure 5: New Server Registration

A dialog window (Figure 6) will come up where you'll specify the server to register and how to connect. If you need to, you can test to verify you can connect successfully before registering the server. Once you click OK, the server will be listed in your Registered Servers list.

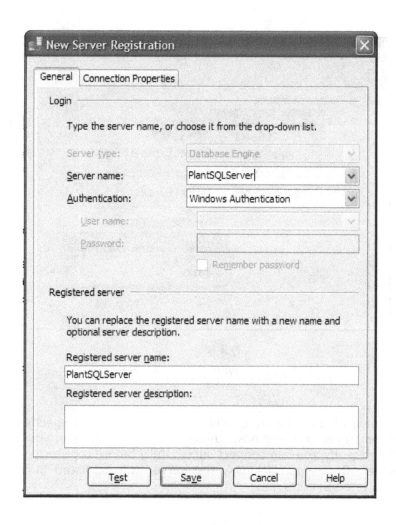

Figure 6: Registered Server Properties

If a server is listed on the Registered Servers list, you can right-click on the server and choose Object Explorer (Figure 7). This will automatically establish the connection to the SQL Server and switch to the Object Explorer where you'll see the server. If you need to enter credentials because the server is registered to connect using SQL Server authentication, then SSMS will prompt you.

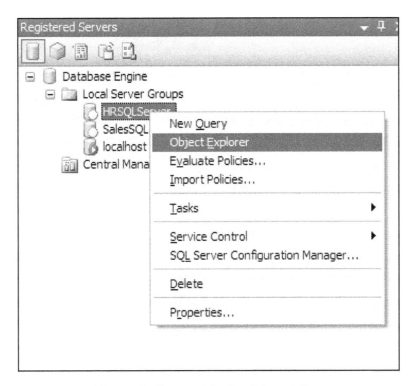

Figure 7: Connect to Registered Server

USING OBJECT EXPLORER

Once we have a server connected in Object Explorer, we can expand the database we want to work with, zero in on a particular table, and right-click on it. This brings up a menu where we can choose to return the first 1000 rows (Figure 8). This is a quick and easy way to begin a SELECT query to return information from a particular table.

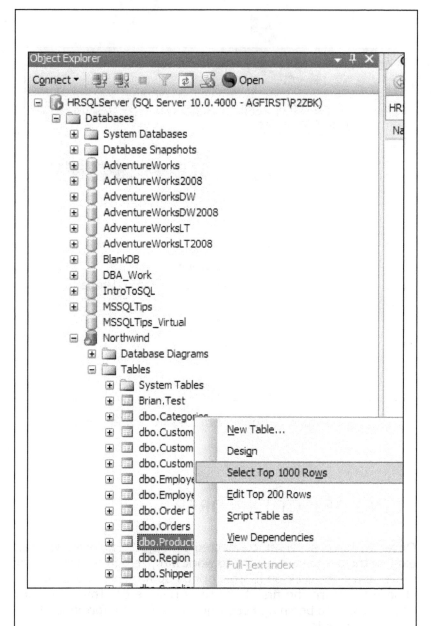

Figure 8: Selecting rows from a table

Once we've returned rows, we can modify the query to be more selective of the columns we want, to add filtering to narrow in and return only the rows matching certain criteria, or we can join two or more tables together to get a complete picture of the data we want. All of these ways of working with the data will be discussed in more detail in later chapters. However, figure 9 gives an example where the top 1000 rows have been returned for the Products table and shows that SSMS even gives us the query used to return the data.

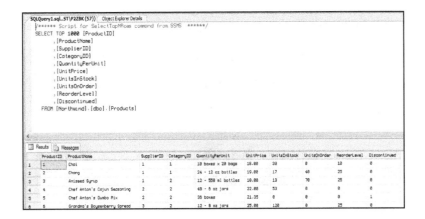

Figure 9: Top 1000 rows returned

If you're not used to the SQL (or Transact-SQL variation of the language used by Microsoft SQL Server), you do have the option of building your query graphically. To do this, make sure the top part of the right hand pane, where the SQL query first appears, is clear, then right-click and choose Design Query in Editor (Figure 10).

Figure 10: Selecting the Query Designer

This will bring up a dialog window where you first will be prompted on what tables/views, etc. to add, as shown in Figure 11.

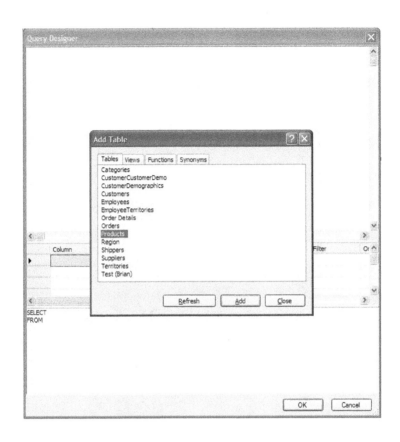

Figure 11: Query Designer Dialog Window

Once you select the table(s) and/or view(s) you want, you then have the option of selecting what columns to include, how to sort the data, and what, if any, filters you want to apply. An example is shown in Figure 12.

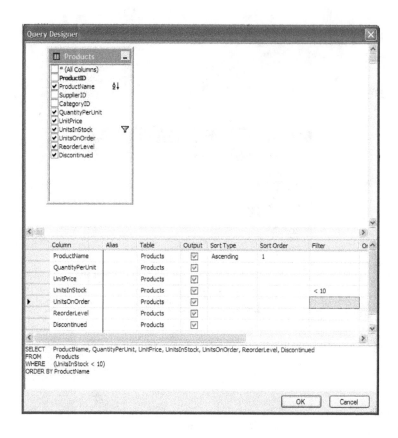

Figure 12: Building the Query

Once the query is built to your satisfaction, you can click OK and SSMS will take you back to where you see the query in the right-hand pane. If you click the Execute button (the button with a red exclamation point), the query will be executed and the results will be displayed, as in Figure 13.

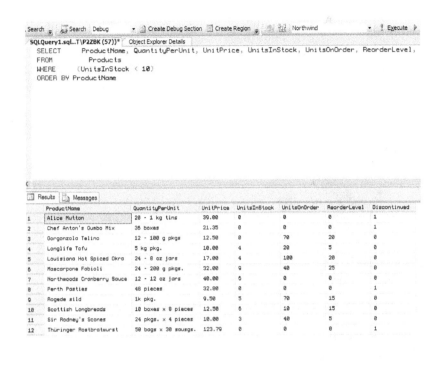

```
.Search   Search  Debug          ▾  Create Debug Section  Create Region     Northwind              ▾   ! Execute  ▸
SQLQuery1.sql...T\P2ZBK (57))*   Object Explorer Details
    SELECT      ProductName, QuantityPerUnit, UnitPrice, UnitsInStock, UnitsOnOrder, ReorderLevel,
    FROM        Products
    WHERE       (UnitsInStock < 10)
    ORDER BY ProductName
```

Results	Messages

	ProductName	QuantityPerUnit	UnitPrice	UnitsInStock	UnitsOnOrder	ReorderLevel	Discontinued
1	Alice Mutton	20 - 1 kg tins	39.00	0	0	0	1
2	Chef Anton's Gumbo Mix	36 boxes	21.35	0	0	0	1
3	Gorgonzola Telino	12 - 100 g pkgs	12.50	0	70	20	0
4	Longlife Tofu	5 kg pkg.	10.00	4	20	5	0
5	Louisiana Hot Spiced Okra	24 - 8 oz jars	17.00	4	100	20	0
6	Mascarpone Fabioli	24 - 200 g pkgs.	32.00	9	40	25	0
7	Northwoods Cranberry Sauce	12 - 12 oz jars	40.00	6	0	0	0
8	Perth Pasties	48 pieces	32.80	0	0	0	1
9	Rogede sild	1k pkg.	9.50	5	70	15	0
10	Scottish Longbreads	10 boxes x 8 pieces	12.50	6	10	15	0
11	Sir Rodney's Scones	24 pkgs. x 4 pieces	10.00	3	40	5	0
12	Thüringer Rostbratwurst	50 bags x 30 sausgs.	123.79	0	0	0	1

Figure 13: Results from the Query

LOADING / SAVING QUERIES

Eventually you will develop queries that you want to save queries that you re-use all the time. To do that, either click on the floppy disk icon on the toolbar (Figure 14) or choose File > Save from the menu (or simply use the shortcut CTRL+S). Make sure the cursor is on the query editor window when you do so.

Figure 14: Open and Save Icons

Retrieving a saved query file is just as easy. Either click on the folder with the arrow pointing away from it on the toolbar (also in Figure 14) or chose File > Open from the menu (the shortcut is CTRL+O). Whether you are saving or opening a query file, the file dialog window which is used by most Windows programs will come up, allowing you to select the path, the filename, etc.

ADD-INS

I mentioned earlier that SSMS allows for add-ins which extend the functionality of SQL Server. One add-in you'll probably want to grab is Mladen Prajdic's SSMS Tools Pack. You can find and download the install at http://www.ssmstoolspack.com/ and it comes with an assortment of useful tools. Some of the functionality you can do with the SSMS Tools Pack is shown in Figure 15.

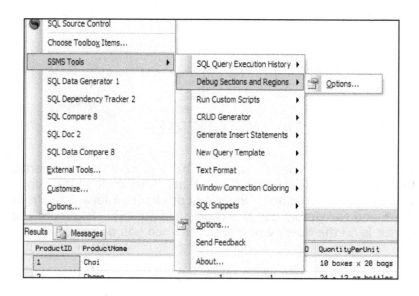

Figure 15: SSMS Tools Pack Add-In

If you are wondering how to get the add-in to display in SSMS, all you need to do is install it. The add-in should register itself properly within SSMS, meaning the next time you start up SQL Server Management Studio after you've installed an add-in it should be present. To remove an add-in, you just go to the Control Panel > Add/Remove Programs and choose to remove the installation of the add-in.

CONCLUSION

In this chapter we did a brief overview of SQL Server Management Studio, a tool that comes with the SQL Server Client Tools installation. It is the de facto tool for most database administrators and developers working with SQL Server due to its power and functionality.

We looked at how to register servers so we don't always have to remember their names, how to begin queries by using the object explorer, how to create queries using the GUI-based Query Designer, and how we save and load those queries for future use. Finally, we looked at add-ins and in particular, the SSMS Tools Pack add-in, which can extend the functionality and power of SQL Server Management Studio.

CHAPTER 4: DATABASE OBJECTS

Now that you can successfully connect to your SQL Server databases, the natural and logical question is "What are you allowed to do?" Your DBA will have assigned your login a set of privileges as to what is permissible. If you have been granted permissions to simply connect to the database and use already existing database objects, then you won't be able to execute many of the object creation commands in this chapter. But you should read this chapter nonetheless to understand what those database objects are.

DATA DEFINITION LANGUAGE

The SQL language has two basic types of commands: those for creating and altering database objects and those for accessing and working with the data in those objects. The CREATE and ALTER commands belong to the first type, and are referred to as DDL for *"Data Definition Language"* statements. The SELECT, INSERT, UPDATE and DELETE belong to the second type, and are known as DML for *"Data Manipulation Language"* statements. In this chapter we'll be covering DDL commands for the basic and most frequently used database objects. Remember, DDL commands require the DBA to have granted you the requisite privileges to perform them.

Note – at the end of this chapter are syntax diagrams for the CREATE and ALTER commands. You may want to bookmark these for future reference.

TABLES

The "*table*" is the key database object. Recall from Chapter 1 that relational databases are required by Codd's rules to store data in tables possessing rows and columns. Thus all relational database management systems must offer tables.

A table is nothing more than a persistent database object or container for your structured data. Structured data simply means that the business recognizes and defines the business objects along with their characteristics or properties. In the old days that would have been a file record layout, now it's the table definition. A table should contain the business data the way the business knows it – and not in some information systems person's idea of the best technical way to do it.

You will want to define multiple varied containers for the different business objects that you work with. So if you work with the business concepts of customers and orders, then you might create CUSTOMER and ORDER tables. Their structure will be different because the business assigns the important characteristics or properties that each must have – which become the columns in a table. Figure 1 shows an example of a simple CREATE TABLE command.

```
CREATE TABLE customer (
    first_name    VARCHAR(20)  NOT NULL,
    last_name     VARCHAR(30)  NOT NULL,
    phone_num     VARCHAR(10),
    street_name   VARCHAR(40),
    city_name     VARCHAR(20),
    state_code    CHAR(2),
    zip_code      CHAR(5)
);
```

Figure 1: CREATE TABLE syntax

The CREATE TABLE command syntax is pretty easy, you simply name the table, define the column names, their data types (including length or size) and whether they are optional or mandatory (i.e. NOT NULL). Figure 2 shows this CREATE TABLE command for the CUSTOMER table executed in SQL Server Management Studio.

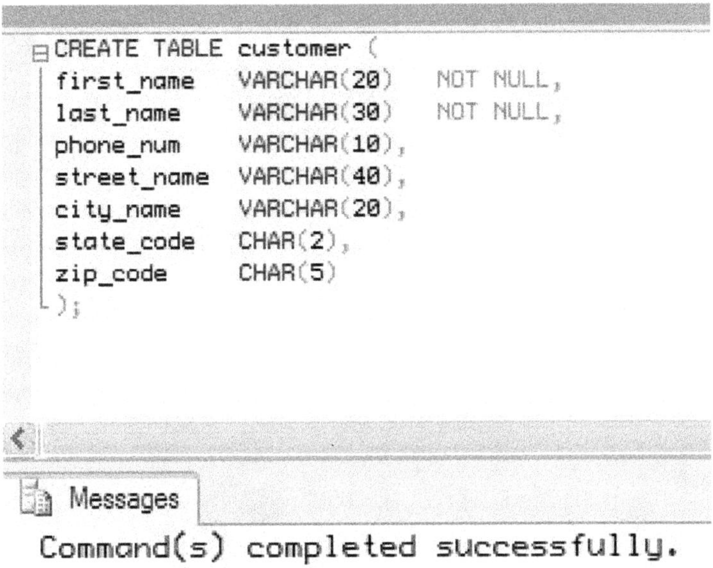

```
CREATE TABLE customer (
    first_name    VARCHAR(20)    NOT NULL,
    last_name     VARCHAR(30)    NOT NULL,
    phone_num     VARCHAR(10),
    street_name   VARCHAR(40),
    city_name     VARCHAR(20),
    state_code    CHAR(2),
    zip_code      CHAR(5)
);
```

Messages

Command(s) completed successfully.

Figure 2: CREATE TABLE executed

Now that you have seen the command syntax and understand what's happening, you would probably like to use a graphical tool, like what is provided in SQL Server Management Studio to accomplish the task much easier and quicker as shown in here Figure 3.

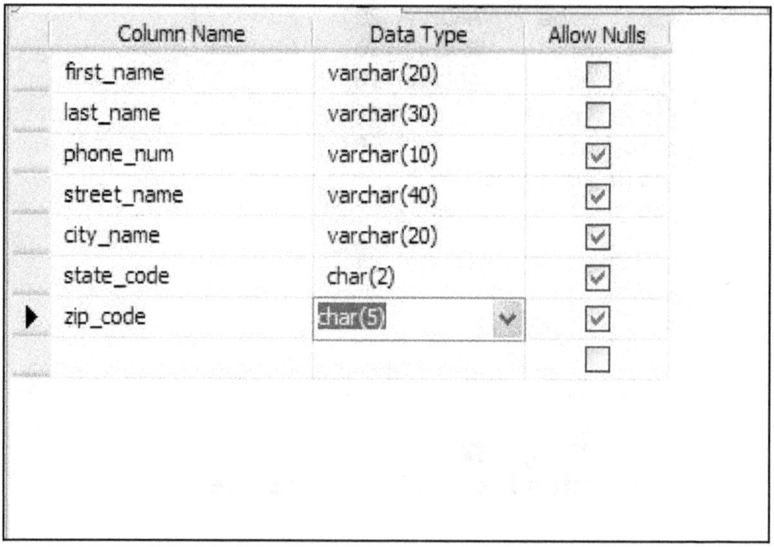

Column Name	Data Type	Allow Nulls
first_name	varchar(20)	☐
last_name	varchar(30)	☐
phone_num	varchar(10)	☑
street_name	varchar(40)	☑
city_name	varchar(20)	☑
state_code	char(2)	☑
▶ zip_code	char(5) ⌄	☑
		☐

Figure 3: Using GUI rather than syntax

Table 1 contains the names and brief description for the more common data types you are likely to need or work with. There are of course many others, reference the SQL Server Books Online for a complete list. There are many more than what are shown here and there have been new additions in SQL Server 2008 and 2008 R2 that weren't in previous versions of Microsoft SQL Server:

CHAR(n)	fixed-length character string that blank-pads to the length n=length
VARCHAR(n)	variable-length character string (no blank padding) n=length
DECIMAL(p,s)	positive & negative numbers with absolute values between 1.0×10^{-38} and 1.0×10^{38} p= total number of decimal digits s= number of digits to the right of the decimal point
INT	integers between -2^{31} and $2^{31}-1$
DATETIME	date and time information: century, year, month, date, hour, minute, second, and milliseconds
NCHAR(n)	fixed-length Unicode character string that blank-pads to the length n=length
NVARCHAR(n)	variable-length Unicode character string (no blank padding) n=length
FLOAT(n)	non-integer numbers that vary in size depending on the value of n. n refers to the number of bits used to store the number. If just float is used (without the parentheses and n), then float(24) is used. For float(24), the number could be from -1.79×10^{308} to 1.79×10^{308}. Float is an approximate value. If you are familiar with significant figures from science, the number of significant figures is either 7 or 15 digits, depending on the size of float(n)

Table 1: Common Data Types

KEY CONSTRAINTS

The next optional step you may perform when creating a table is to define primary and/or unique key constraints. Note too that you can also embed such constraint definitions in the CREATE TABLE statement itself such that they exist from creation time forward – so that no one inserts an data before the constraints are in place. Refer back to Chapter 1 for a description of the differences between key constraints and indexes – one implements a business rule and the other is a database mechanism for quick access.

So let's say the business tells you that no two customers can have the same first name, last name and phone number. Thus every customer can be uniquely recognized and identified by the combination of these three pieces of information. To effect that change you would have to alter the table – and you'd have to make two changes.

Since no part of a primary or unique key can be optional (technically, in SQL Server while a primary key cannot have any optional values, a unique key can have a single NULL, or optional, value but it's still not a good idea), first you must make the phone number a required column. And second, you need to define the primary key constraint on the concatenation of those three columns. Figure 4 shows the ALTER TABLE commands that are required.

```
ALTER TABLE customer
    ALTER COLUMN phone_num
        VARCHAR(10) NOT NULL;

ALTER TABLE customer
    ADD CONSTRAINT PK_Customer
    PRIMARY KEY
        (first_name, last_name, phone_num);
```

Figure 4: ALTER TABLE syntax

INDEXES

The next and final optional step you may perform when creating a table is to define indexes. Maybe either the business tells you or just know from experience that users will often search this table on the state code – and they want fast access based on it. Thus you will need to create an index on that table and column as shown here in Figure 5.

```
CREATE INDEX cust_index2
    ON customer (phone_num);
```

Figure 5: CREATE INDEX syntax

So why was this index named as the second customer index? Because we know that key constraints are implemented via indexes and the prior primary key constraint created the first index on this table. So as shown in Figure 6, SQL Server Management Studio shows that the table has two indexes: one with three columns for the constraint that the system named for us, and the named one specifically created.

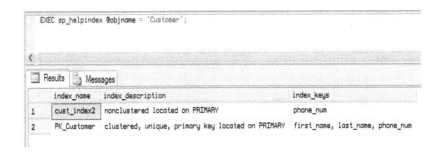

Figure 6: Indexes on Table

VIEWS

A view is nothing more than a subset of or "*picture window*" into one or more tables' columns. If the employee table has a salary column, that might be considered sensitive or privileged data. Thus managers might be able to access the table and all its columns, but employees are only supposed to see the columns minus salary. For that we can create a view as shown in Figure 7 and have non-managers access employee data via the view. While SQL Server can control access on each column, it's often easier to use a view to present only the data we want a given user to see.

```
CREATE TABLE employee (
     emp_num        INTEGER       NOT NULL,
     first_name     VARCHAR(20)   NOT NULL,
     last_name      VARCHAR(30)   NOT NULL,
     salary         DECIMAL(8,2)  NOT NULL,
     phone_num      VARCHAR(10),
     street_name    VARCHAR(40),
     city_name      VARCHAR(20),
     state_code     CHAR(2),
     zip_code       CHAR(5)
);
CREATE VIEW emp_view
AS
SELECT emp_num, first_name,
            last_name, phone_num,
            street_name, city_name,
            state_code, zip_code
FROM employee;
```

Figure 7: CREATE VIEW syntax

The SELECT command is something new and covered more thoroughly in a later chapter. For now, this SELECT is simply informing SQL Server that when you work with the EMP_VIEW view that you are limited to seeing all the EMPLOYEE table columns but salary.

There is another reason why views are so useful (besides the security aspect). What if the business defines a query or report and wants to make sure that all database users always enter the correct command syntax? For example, if the employee name must always show up on reports and screens as last name, comma, first name – then a view such as the one in Figure 8 can address that need.

```
CREATE VIEW emp_view2 (
    emp_num, full_name, phone_num,
    street_name, city_name,
    state_code, zip_code
)
AS
SELECT emp_num, last_name + ',' +
        first_name, phone_num,
        street_name, city_name,
        state_code, zip_code
FROM employee;
```

Figure 8: Complex View syntax

This view command is a little more complex. Since we want to essentially create a new, virtual column on the fly, we have to name the columns as if we're doing a create table command. That's where **full_name** comes from. Then we have to tell the database what columns we want as with any view, plus we have to instruct SQL Server on how to construct that virtual column. That's where the expression **last_name + ',' + first_name** comes from. The two new syntax items here are the concatenation operator + and a literal string, which are characters enclosed in quotes. Do note, that when the + character is used for two number values, it functions as the plus sign in addition. However, for strings it performs string concatenation.

Finally an advanced and very powerful use for views is creating a single view definition that "*glues together*" or "*joins*" multiple related tables (refer to Chapter 6 for more about joins). Thus if users always need to query multiple tables together to correctly see the whole and true "*business picture*", then one can create a view to make those multiple tables appear as one. In other words it lets one hide the physical table design from the business reality.

CONCLUSION

In this chapter learned what the basic database objects are plus some of their CREATE AND ALTER commands. These types of commands as generally referred to as DDL for Data Definition Language – and they often require your DBA to have granted you the rights to perform them. While the tables, constraints, indexes and views discussed in this chapter are a tiny subset of the overall database objects offered these days, they are nonetheless the ones used most often. Thus a fundamental knowledge of these base database objects is often sufficient to begin working with your SQL Server databases.

SYNTAX CHARTS

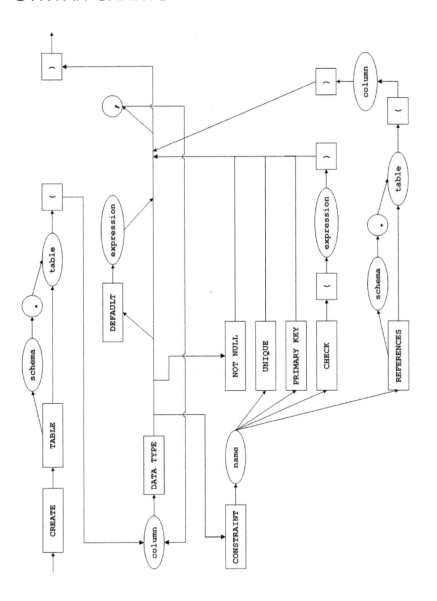

Figure 9: CREATE TABLE

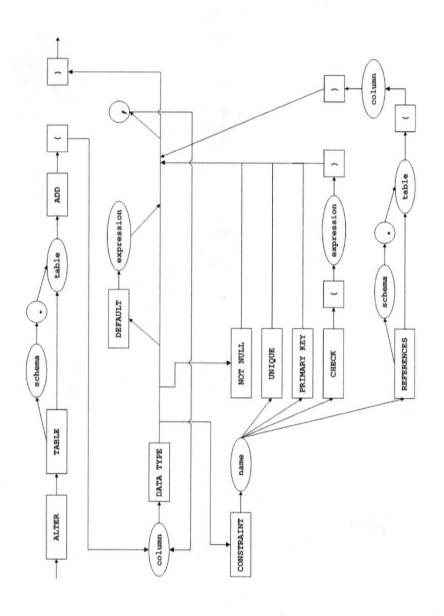

Figure 10: ALTER TABLE - ADD

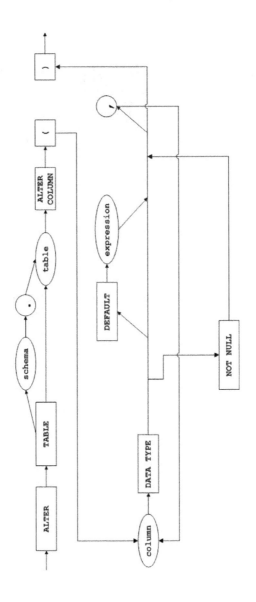

Figure 11: ALTER TABLE - MODIFY

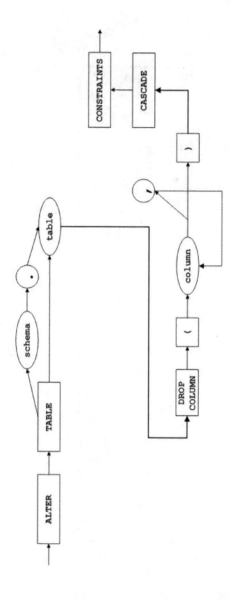

Figure 12: ALTER TABLE - DROP/RENAME

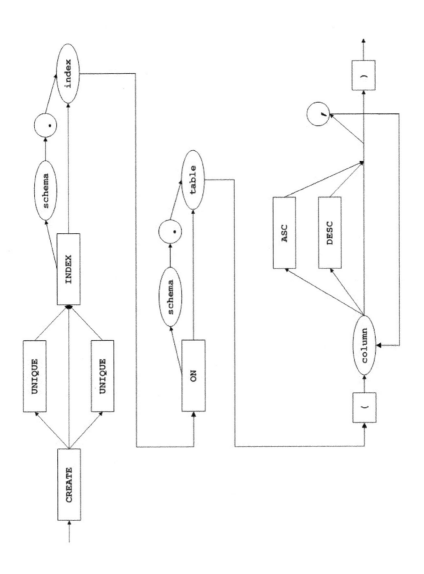

Figure 13: CREATE INDEX

CHAPTER 5: BASIC SQL

The first four chapters have taken you from defining SQL Server, to connecting with the database and creating some rudimentary database objects. Thus it's now time to begin learning the SQL or Structured Query Language. There are four Data Manipulation Language (i.e. DML) commands and three transaction control commands. Even if you will never type these commands per se, you will need to understand their nature. Because even when you use a graphical tool like SQL Server Management Studio, Apex's ApexSQL Edit, Quest Software's TOAD, Microsoft Excel or Microsoft Access, the actions that you'll be performing graphically will be based upon these basic SQL commands.

BEGIN TRANSACTION

The first transactional command is BEGIN TRANSACTION, or BEGIN TRAN, for short. This tells SQL Server that you want to group the following commands together. Either all succeed, or none do. The syntax is as follows:

BEGIN TRAN{SACTION}

If you're used to Oracle, for instance, this represents a change in behavior. By default, SQL Server treats each individual statement as its own transaction. So if you had an UPDATE followed by an INSERT statement (more on both of these later in the chapter), SQL Server would treat these as two individual transactions. One could succeed and the other could fail.

This may not be what we want. For instance, you might have two UPDATE operations for banking. Say you're transferring money from checking to savings. If the first UPDATE statement deducts money from your checking account and the second UPDATE statement puts the money into your savings accounts, you would never want the situation where the deduction from checking happens without the addition to savings also occurring. Likewise, the bank doesn't want the opposite! The key is to wrap the two statements together in a transaction. BEGIN TRAN does that.

COMMIT

The second transactional command is COMMIT, which allows one to post changes to the database for the existing transaction. The syntax is as follows:

COMMIT { WORK | TRAN }

Where the word WORK or TRAN (or TRANSACTION) is optional, but permitted so as to adhere to the ANSI SQL standard or to mirror the BEGIN TRAN statement which starts the transaction in the first place.

ROLLBACK

The final transactional command is ROLLBACK. The syntax is as follows:

ROLLBACK { WORK | TRAN }

Where the word WORK or TRAN (or TRANSACTION) is optional, but permitted so as to adhere to the ANSI SQL standard or mirror the BEGIN TRAN command.

ROLLBACK is pretty much just the opposite of a COMMIT, which is that all of a transaction's interim work is simply undone or thrown away. Since the actions were never committed to the database, no one has ever seen the end results. Think of it as the "*I've changed my mind*" command.

Using the spreadsheet analogy, assume that you open a spreadsheet file and make changes. If another user now opens that file they do not see your changes. If you "save" the file and now the second person opens it, your changes would now be visible or committed. If you instead had closed Excel and chosen not to save your work, now the spreadsheet file is back to the exact same state as when you opened it – or rolled back.

INSERT

The first DML command is INSERT, which allows one to create or add new rows to a table. The basic syntax is:

INSERT INTO table_name

VALUES (value_1 {, value_2, value_3, ... })

There generally will be one value listed per column in the table. Thus you need to know what the table looks like or its structure in order to know the number and kind of values to enter. Figure 1 shows a CREATE TABLE statement followed by five INSERT command examples for that table.

```
CREATE TABLE people (
    rec_no    INTEGER     NOT NULL,
    name      VARCHAR(30) NOT NULL,
    city      VARCHAR(20),
    state     CHAR(2)
);
INSERT INTO people VALUES
    (1,'John Wayne','Dallas','TX');
INSERT INTO people VALUES
    (2,'Clark Gable','Fort Worth','TX');
INSERT INTO people VALUES
    (3,'Errol Flynn','Austin','TX');
INSERT INTO people VALUES
    (4,'Betty Davis', NULL, NULL);
INSERT INTO people VALUES
    (5,'Gina Davis');
```

Figure 1: INSERT Examples

The first three INSERT examples in Figure 1 look pretty much as expected. Note though that the fourth INSERT uses the special NULL keyword – which means empty or no value. Since the city and state columns were defined as being optional, you do not have to provide a real value for them to the INSERT command.

But look at the fifth INSERT which tries to entirely skip providing those two values. The database will report the "*not enough values*" error. So the NULL keyword serves as the placeholder to tell the database no value, and it has to be there even for an optional column. It is possible in SQL Server to specify the values for like in the fifth INSERT statement, but the catch is you must tell SQL Server exactly what columns are affected. So if that last INSERT is modified to the following (Figure 2), it will work:

```
INSERT INTO people (rec_no, Name)
      VALUES (5, 'Gina Davis');
```

Figure 2: Corrected INSERT Statement

DELETE

The second DML command is DELETE, which allows one to drop existing rows from a table. The basic syntax is:

DELETE FROM table_name

{ WHERE condition(s) }

Note that the WHERE clause portion of the command is optional. But be careful, as a DELETE command without the WHERE condition will drop every row from the table – making it empty. So in most cases you should include some kind of WHERE conditions. Figure 3 shows a few examples:

```
DELETE FROM people
   WHERE rec_no = 1;
DELETE FROM people
   WHERE state = 'TX';
DELETE FROM people
   WHERE city IS NULL;
DELETE from people
   WHERE city = 'Dallas' OR
         city = 'Fort Worth';
DELETE FROM people
   WHERE name LIKE '%n%';
```

Figure 3: DELETE Examples

Using the five rows that were inserted previously in Figure 1 and Figure 2, the five DELETE commands in Figure 3 would behave individually as follows:

- Deletes one record: John Wayne

- Deletes three records: everyone except Betty Davis and Gina Davis

- Deletes two records: Betty Davis and Gina Davis

- Deletes two records: John Wayne and Clark Gable

- Deletes three records: John Wayne, Eroll Flynn, and Gina Davis

Note the special syntax of the last three DELETE examples' WHERE clauses. Let's examine them closer and understand these special WHERE clause syntaxes.

In the third DELETE example, when you want to specify to the database an empty value as part of the WHERE clause there are two requirements. First, as with the INSERT command, you need to use the special NULL keyword. Second and most critical, when using NULL in a WHERE clause you must use "IS NULL" or "IS NOT NULL". The equal sign will not function as expected with

NULL values. Had you said WHERE city = NULL, the database would return zero rows.

In the fourth DELETE example, note that you can write multiple conditions that must be met and connect them with the conditional operators of "AND" and "OR". Furthermore just as you might write a more complex mathematical expression, you can include parenthesis to clarify and control the conditions' order of precedence. In fact for readability for the next person who may have to look at your SQL, it's advisable to generally include parenthesis.

In the fifth DELETE example, note the new operator "LIKE" and the special meta character "%". LIKE equates to the concept of contains, so in this case the person's name has an "n" in it. Plus that "n" can be anywhere in the string as indicated by the "%", which is simply the wildcard character. Most people are probably more familiar with the asterisk or "*" being the wildcard, but in SQL Server it's the percent sign. If we had instead wanted to delete people whose name begin with "J" then the syntax would have been WHERE name LIKE 'J%'.

UPDATE

The third DML command is UPDATE, which allows one to modify column values for existing rows in a table. The basic syntax is:

UPDATE FROM table_name

SET column_1 = value_1,

{, column_2 = value_2, ... }

{ WHERE condition(s) }

Note that the WHERE clause portion of the command is optional. But be careful, as an UPDATE command without the WHERE condition will modify every row in the table – thus performing a global change. So in most cases you should include some kind of WHERE conditions. Figure 4 shows a few examples:

```
UPDATE people
   SET city = 'Houston'
   WHERE rec_no = 1;
UPDATE people
   SET city  = 'Atlanta',
       state = 'GA'
   WHERE state = 'TX';
UPDATE people
   SET city  = 'Tampa',
       state = 'FL'
   WHERE city IS NULL;
UPDATE people
   SET city  = 'Phoenix',
       state = 'AZ'
   WHERE city = 'Dallas' OR
         city = 'Fort Worth';
UPDATE people
   SET city = 'El Paso'
   WHERE name LIKE '%n%';
```

Figure 4: UPDATE Examples

Using the five rows that were inserted previously in Figure 1 and Figure 2, the five UPDATE commands in Figure 4 would behave individually as follows:

- Updates one record: relocated to John Wayne to Houston
- Updates three records: everyone except Betty Davis and Gina Davis relocated to Atlanta
- Updates two records: Betty Davis and Gina Davis relocated to Tampa
- Updates two records: John Wayne and Clark Gable relocated to Phoenix
- Updates three records: John Wayne, Eroll Flynn, and Gina Davis relocated to El Paso

Note the special syntax of the last three UPDATE examples'
WHERE clauses. They function identically as was described in
the prior section for the DELETE command. Refer back to that
section for a better description.

SELECT

The fourth and final DML command is SELECT, which allows one
to retrieve and display existing rows from a table. The basic
syntax is:

> SELECT
>
>   * | column_1 { , column_2 ... }
>
>   FROM table_name
>
>   { WHERE condition(s) }

Note that the WHERE clause portion of the command is optional.
But be careful, as a SELECT command without the WHERE
condition will return every row in the table – so all ten billion rows
from a huge table. Since that data has to traverse the network
to get to you, you'll tax the network. And in some cases your
software and/or PC may not be able to handle the return of that
much data – either crashing and/or returning "*insufficient or out
of memory*" errors. So in most cases you should include some
kind of WHERE conditions.

We're going to incrementally develop SELECT command examples
because SELECT is the single most frequently used SQL command.
Figure 5 shows the most basic form: SELECT * FROM table_name,
which simply retrieves all the columns (i.e. *) and all the rows
(i.e. no WHERE clause) for the table.

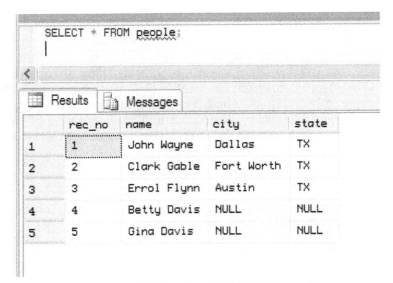

Figure 5: Simplest SELECT Example

One of the strengths of relational databases is that they are built upon a mathematical foundation, known as relational algebra and relational calculus. Hence everything can be expressed mathematically – and thus one can construct mathematical proofs as to the command's accuracy. We won't go into that other than to say that the relational terms for the SELECT command fall into two categories: projection and restriction.

Projection simply means what columns does the SELECT command display as per the second line of the syntax (i.e. * | column_1 { , column_2 ... }). Thus the asterisk (i.e. *) means project or display all the columns, whereas naming the columns yourself means to project or display just those. Think of projection as what columns of data for from table do I need back from the database in order to accomplish the task at hand. Returning to our spreadsheet analogy, if you cut and paste a range of columns from one worksheet to another then you've performed a "*projection*".

Restriction simply means what rows does the SELECT command display as per the fourth line of the syntax (i.e. WHERE clause). Thus no WHERE clause means no restriction or display all the rows, whereas specifying a WHERE clause means to restrict display just the rows that meet the criteria. Think of restriction as what rows of data for from table do I need back from the database in order to accomplish the task at hand. Returning to our spreadsheet analogy, if you cut and paste a range of rows from one worksheet to another then you've performed a *"restriction"*.

Figure 6 shows a more complex and complete SELECT command using all the things we've learned so far.

```
SELECT name, city, state
    FROM people
    WHERE city = 'Dallas' OR
          state = 'TX';
```

Figure 6: Complete SELECT Example

This SELECT example performs both user specified projections and restrictions. Thus this example is much more like the command that you'll be writing. The results for this SELECT are shown here in Figure 7.

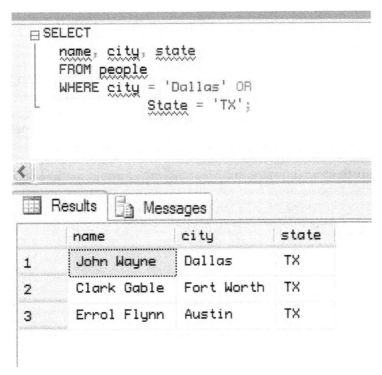

```
☐ SELECT
    name, city, state
    FROM people
    WHERE city = 'Dallas' OR
              State = 'TX';
```

◁

	name	city	state
1	John Wayne	Dallas	TX
2	Clark Gable	Fort Worth	TX
3	Errol Flynn	Austin	TX

Figure 7: Complete SELECT Output

A note about returning data using SELECT. You'll typically want to ensure that you return only what you need. This means avoiding the use of * and explicitly stating the columns, like what was done in Figure 6. This ensures that the amount of traffic over the network is kept to a minimum, thus returning your queries quicker. It also prevents an issue if the table gets modified, say a column gets added that you weren't prepared to handle.

While SELECT is the most frequently used SQL command, it's also is the most complex. However in this chapter we learned just the very basics. The SELECT command will be covered more thoroughly in the chapter for Advanced SQL. What we've covered in this chapter is probably 10% of what the SELECT command syntax has to offer.

CONCLUSION

In this chapter we covered the most basic SQL commands and their syntax. We've built upon all that we've learned so far to actually INSERT, DELETE, UPDATE and SELECT data from tables. Plus we learned how to wrap data changes in a transaction (i.e. BEGIN TRAN and COMMIT) or undo what has been currently modified in a transaction (i.e. ROLLBACK). With just these basics you now have a fundamental working knowledge of the SQL language, and thus how to work with your databases. It would be worth stopping here and "*test driving*" what you now know on your database before proceeding. Because next we're going to take this knowledge to the next level – and that's about ten times more complex than this material. Some experience is thus advisable.

CHAPTER 6: ADVANCED SQL

The last chapter went over the six basic SQL commands that you'll use most often – but just in their simplest forms. Now we'll incrementally delve into more complex versions of the SELECT command and thereby answer more complex business questions. Again you may not end up writing such SELECT commands, but rather using some graphical tool to communicate your desires and having it generate the SQL. But you'll need to understand this chapter's concepts in order to comprehend and therefore utilize those graphical representations.

NOTE: This chapter's sections and examples are each added to the basic SELECT syntax to keep things easy. At the end there are examples showing how all these individual constructs can be utilized together to form highly complex SELECT statements.

ORDER BY

When you SELECT data from a table, the database engine is free to return the records or rows in whatever manner is most expedient – often in an order that has nothing to do with any business criteria. Thus if you want the rows returned sorted by some meaningful business characteristics, you must instruct the database to sort the rows before returning them to you. For that the basic SELECT syntax is expanded upon as follows (with the new clause indicated in bold).

SELECT

   * | column_1 { , column_2 ... }

   FROM table_name

   { WHERE condition(s) }

   { ORDER BY

      column_1 {<u>ASC</u>|DESC}

   { ,column_2 {<u>ASC</u>|DESC}... }}

Note that you can sort by one or more columns and optionally in ascending or descending order per column, with ascending being the default. Figure 1 shows an example of sorting by the city column of the people table developed in the last chapter.

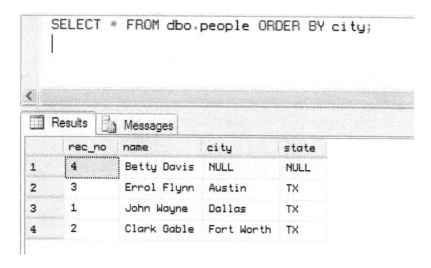

Figure 1: ORDER BY Example

The ORDER BY clause introduces a measurable performance penalty as the database engine must first gather all the desired rows, then sort and return them. Of course the more data expected to be returned the larger the performance penalty. But if you need the data in a guaranteed order, you must add the ORDER BY clause.

Note: Sometimes the database will by sheer luck seemingly return the rows in sorted order. But only utilizing the ORDER BY clause can guarantee this.

GROUP BY

Sometimes the business question at hand requires one row of output for each grouping of similar rows. For example you might want to know how many people live in each state. But if you just try a GROUP BY with a simple SELECT * you'll get an error shown here in Figure 2 (trimmed to show the start of the error) indicating that a column in the select list isn't contained in an aggregate function or in the GROUP BY clause.

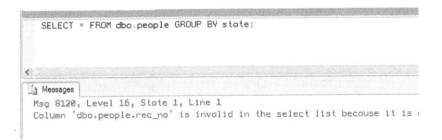

Figure 2: GROUP BY Error

Whenever you use a GROUP BY clause there are generally three additional requirements: the projection criteria (what SQL Server calls the select list - the columns you are asking for in your SELECT query) must include a "group" or aggregate function (such as SUM() to add up the values or COUNT() to return how many values), the GROUP BY clause must specify the columns construct groupings for, and often the projection criteria will also include the same columns as the GROUP BY clause – that way you have a meaningful column of data to go with each of the group function row results. Figure 3 shows the correct syntax for querying how many people live in each state.

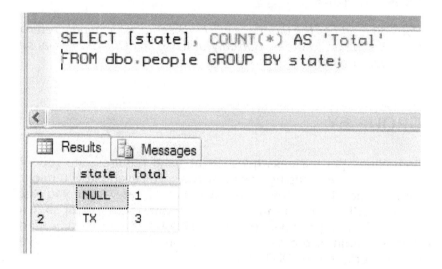

Figure 3: GROUP BY Row Example

Note the first row of output – there's one person whose state is NULL. The second rows shows that there are 3 people whose state is Texas. When constructing typical business queries and reports, you'll use the GROUP BY syntax often. It's a very powerful tool.

So what are these "group" functions? They are functions returning one value when applied to the columns specified for that grouping. The asterisk (i.e. *) simply means to use the entire record as the grouping column. In Figure 3 the COUNT(*) grouping function was used to simply count how many rows of people occur per unique state value. In many cases you'll specify a column like shown here in Figure 4.

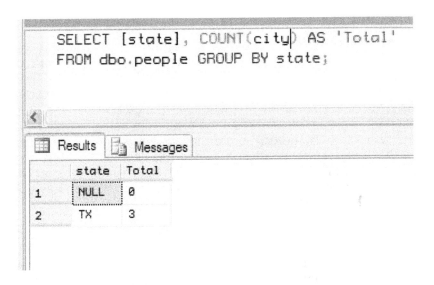

```
SELECT [state], COUNT(city) AS 'Total'
FROM dbo.people GROUP BY state;
```

	state	Total
1	NULL	0
2	TX	3

Figure 4: GROUP BY Column Example

There are many group functions, but the ones you'll at first and most often include:

- AVG

- COUNT

- MAX

- MIN

- STDDEV

- SUM

Did you notice the seemingly odd difference for the NULL records between Figure 3 and Figure 4? Figure 3 shows one record for the NULL state, but Figure 4 shows zero. Why are they different? Remember that you must use IS NULL and IS NOT NULL in WHERE clauses because NULL's do not behave the way you might expect. The same is true when you apply any function to a NULL value – the result is always zero!

HAVING

The HAVING clause is actually very simple in concept, but it's quite often considered one of the seemingly more confusing features. The WHERE clause performs restrictions at the row level and thus eliminates table rows from being included. Whereas the HAVING clause performs restrictions at the group level and thus eliminates group function resulting rows from being included. So the WHERE clause occurs before the group function whereas the HAVING clause occurs after. Knowing this simple fact alone can often help you to decide when to use one clause versus the other. In other words, think of the HAVING clause as the same as the filter for the GROUP BY clause.

So how can we modify the query in Figure 4 to only include those results where the city count is greater than zero and thus eliminate that first, kind of meaningless row? That's exactly what the HAVING clause is for, and the syntax would be like that shown in Figure 5.

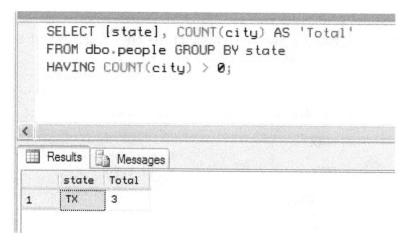

Figure 5: HAVING Example

Finally note that while the GROUP BY creates groupings, it doesn't automatically sort their output order. So if multiple grouping rows are to be returned and you want them sorted, you must also use the ORDER BY clause. A common mistake is to assume that the

GROUP BY clause somehow does both and to leave the ORDER BY clause off.

DISTINCT

Sometimes you may need to know what the range or universe of existing values are for a column. For example we may want to know what cities exist within the people table. For that we need to use the DISTINCT clause as shown here in Figure 6.

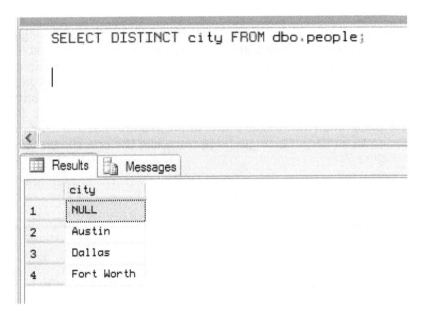

Figure 6: DISTINCT Example

The DISTINCT clause introduces a measurable performance penalty as the database engine must first gather all the desired rows, sort them and then return one value per group. Of course the more data expected to be returned the larger the performance penalty. But if you need to know the list of unique values for a column, then consider utilizing the DISTINCT clause.

However always make sure that your need is genuine and that DISTINCT is the only or best way to solve the problem. Because the DISTINCT clause is probably the most overused SELECT construct – very often used as a crutch when the problem and the efficient SQL for it are a little less obvious. In these cases people will often fall back or resort to use the DISTINCT clause to quickly (but very inefficiently) dig them out of a SQL coding quandary.

JOINS

Thus far all the SELECT examples have operated upon a single table, hence the FROM clauses have each listed just one table. However optimal relational design often adheres to the principles of *"data normalization"*, which simply means to break the data up into more smaller but related tables to reduce data redundancy – which should then translate into more accurate data. But it's not uncommon for those more familiar with *"flat file"* record design to construct a single large table like the one shown here in Figure 7.

```
CREATE TABLE Products (
    ProductID      INT            NOT NULL,
    ProductName    VARCHAR(40)    NOT NULL,
    CategoryName   VARCHAR(15)    NOT NULL,
    CategoryDesc   VARCHAR(200)       NULL
    UnitPrice      DECIMAL(7,2)   NOT NULL,
    UnitsInStock   SMALLINT       NOT NULL
```

Figure 7: Poor Table Design

Which results in data like shown here in Figure 8.

	ProductID	ProductName	CategoryName	CategoryDesc	UnitPrice	UnitsInStock
1	1	Chai	Beverages	Soft drinks, coff...	18.00	39
2	2	Chang	Beverages	Soft drinks, coff...	19.00	17
3	3	Aniseed Syrup	Condiments	Sweet and savory ...	10.00	13
4	4	Chef Anton's Cajun...	Condiments	Sweet and savory ...	22.00	53
5	5	Chef Anton's Gumbo...	Condiments	Sweet and savory ...	21.35	0
6	6	Grandma's Boysenbe...	Condiments	Sweet and savory ...	25.00	120
7	7	Uncle Bob's Organi...	Produce	Dried fruit and b...	30.00	15
8	8	Northwoods Cranber...	Condiments	Sweet and savory ...	40.00	6

Figure 8: Poor Table Data

There are two problems with this table design and its data. First, the fact that the CategoryDesc (abbreviated for Category Description) is repeated once for every product in the appropriate Category. Thus to modify the Category Description you'd have to update every product in that category. So what if the Beverages category had 50,000 products – that update could take a while. Second, what if the update accidentally missed some of those product records? Then we'd have a business quandary whereby a category would have multiple descriptions. It's this second problem that will almost always occur over time, and hence why normalizing table designs is such a critical concept.

Thus the more relationally correct and preferred design would be to split this big table into two smaller related tables as shown here by Figure 9. Since the category ID, name and description only depend upon the category ID, those columns are split off into a separate table. The category ID is then left in the product table as a logical pointer known as the foreign key (refer back to Chapter 1 for the definition and Chapter 4 for the create table syntax).

```
CREATE TABLE Categories (
    CategoryID    INT            NOT NULL,
    CategoryName  VARCHAR(15)    NOT NULL,
    CategoryDesc  VARCHAR(50)        NULL
);

CREATE TABLE Products (
    ProductID     INT            NOT NULL,
    ProductName   VARCHAR(40     NOT NULL,
    CategoryID    INT            NOT NULL,
    UnitPrice     DECIMAL(7,2)   NOT NULL,
    UnitsInStock  SMALLINT       NOT NULL
);
```

Figure 9: Correct Table Design

Therefore with many smaller, properly normalized and related table designs, you'll quite often need to glue together or "*join*" one or more of those related tables to construct the full or complete business data that you're after. In other words you'll need to project from more than one table to construct the desired and complete output. For that the basic SELECT syntax is expanded upon as follows (with the new clauses indicated in bold).

```
SELECT
  {table|alias.}* |
  {table|alias.}column_1
  { , {table|alias.}column_2 ... }
FROM table_1 {{AS} alias_1}
{ , table_2 {{AS} alias_2} ... }
{ WHERE
    {{table_1|alias.}column_1 =
      {table_2|alias.}column_2
    ...}
  { AND condition(s) } }
```

The above syntax is referred to as the *"implicit"* JOIN SQL coding style. It is considered by many as legacy and out of vogue. However it is still commonly used by people and many software tools generate their SQL code in this style – so it's still wise to be able to read it. Using our properly designed (i.e. normalized) EMP and DEPT tables from Figure 9, here's the implicit JOIN syntax to display the same output as in Figure 8 that was based upon the one big and poorly designed table. Examine it closely – there is quite a lot going on in this one simple example.

```
SELECT p.*, c.categoryname,
        c.categorydesc
FROM Products p, Categories c
WHERE p.CategoryID = c.CategoryID;
```

Figure 10: Implicit JOIN Example

One golden rule when doing any join is to make sure that you specify the proper number and type of join conditions. There should be a join condition between the parent primary key and the child foreign key for the table count minus one listed in the FROM clause. Moreover if those keys are composites (i.e. have multiple columns), then there will also be a additional condition per that key column count. If you skip the join conditions altogether or even just incorrectly specify them, the database will by default perform a "*Cartesian JOIN*" or a CROSS JOIN – which is simply every row from one table mindlessly joined to every row from the other. You almost never, ever want such a join because there is no real business logic or rationale for these row combinations. So always avoid a Cartesian JOIN unless the circumstances really require it! There are rare cases, like in genetics where you're working with alleles and Punnett squares, but in all other cases you should be suspicious if you see one.

One sure way to avoid a Cartesian JOIN due to mistakes in the query is to use the newer and preferred ASNI JOIN syntax. For that the basic SELECT syntax is expanded upon as follows (with the new clauses indicated in bold).

SELECT
    {table|alias.}* |
    {table|alias.}column_1
    { , {table|alias.}column_2 ... }
    FROM table_1 {{AS} alias_1}
    { {INNER |
      {FULL|LEFT|RIGHT} OUTER}
      JOIN
      table_2 {{AS} alias_2} ON
      { table_1|alias.}column_1 =
        {table_2|alias.}column_2
      ...}
    ... }
    { WHERE condition(s) } }

The above syntax is referred to as the "*explicit*" JOIN SQL coding style. Since the WHERE conditions and JOIN logic are now separated, it becomes a little clearer during SQL coding as to what is needed and when. Note the optional **INNER** keyword. By default database joins combine only the rows from both sides or tables that fully satisfy the join condition expressions. Any rows from either side or table that fail to meet those conditions are excluded.

Say you want to see the category names and their product counts, but only for those categories that have products currently listed in them. Therefore an inner join between Products and Categories is needed as shown below in Figure 11. Note that this example uses both the INNER JOIN and GROUP BY features of the SELECT statement. We've now reached the point where doing anything useful with a SELECT command is going to require using multiple syntactical features. That's all right because in reality that's the type of SQL code you most often be writing.

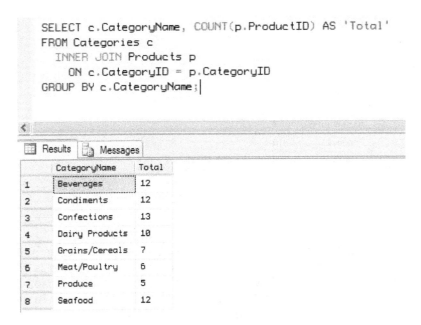

Figure 11: INNER JOIN Example

But there is an interesting business question here – do these results tell the whole story? Maybe you really wanted to see the category names and their product counts for all categories no matter what – even if no products are currently listed. Therefore an outer join between Categories and Products is needed as shown below in Figure 12.

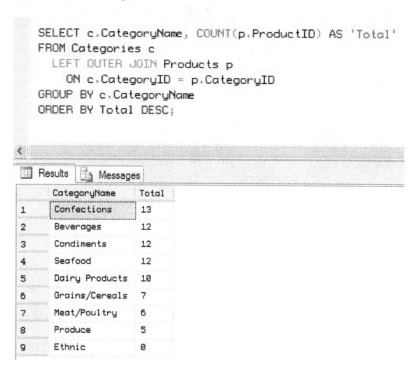

```
SELECT c.CategoryName, COUNT(p.ProductID) AS 'Total'
FROM Categories c
  LEFT OUTER JOIN Products p
    ON c.CategoryID = p.CategoryID
GROUP BY c.CategoryName
ORDER BY Total DESC;
```

	CategoryName	Total
1	Confections	13
2	Beverages	12
3	Condiments	12
4	Seafood	12
5	Dairy Products	10
6	Grains/Cereals	7
7	Meat/Poultry	6
8	Produce	5
9	Ethnic	0

Figure 12: OUTER JOIN Example

The fact that there is a category Ethnic and that no products are listed might be critical information. Hence the outer join is the more business correct way to write this query as it exposes all the truth. Therefore think about what the business needs to see or know as you write your joins, you may find that in many cases the outer join is the better choice. There is a popular myth that outer joins are less efficient or slower than inner joins. They are not. Besides who cares – even if they were slower, the right answer is what's needed.

So what do the LEFT (as in Figure 12), RIGHT and FULL OUTER JOIN qualifiers do? They simply specify which side of the JOIN or table to include even if there are no matching rows from the other side or table. Therefore in Figure 12 LEFT simply means to include the DEPT rows even though no employees may work there. In other words include left side rows no matter what. FULL would simply include both sides (i.e. the equivalent of specifying both LEFT and RIGHT at the same time).

SUB-SELECT'S

Thus far all the SELECT command examples are merely but a single, simple select operation. Even with JOIN's and all the other advanced syntax, there is still just one select operation being performed per command. But there are times when you may need to nest one SELECT operation within another – known as sub-SELECT's or sub queries. For that the basic SELECT syntax is expanded upon as follows (with the new clause indicated in bold).

```
SELECT ...
FROM ...
WHERE ...
    condition =|IN (SELECT ...)
{ AND condition(s) } }
{ GROUP BY ... }
{ HAVING ... }
{ ORDER BY ...}
```

This expanded syntax supports answering business questions like what is the average unit price in the category that has the most products? Let's construct this sub-query incrementally starting with the query shown in here Figure 13, which simply returns the total number of products (in the entire catalog and thus all categories), and their average unit price.

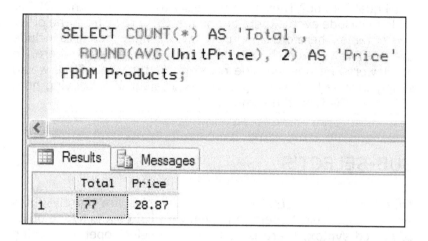

```
SELECT COUNT(*) AS 'Total',
    ROUND(AVG(UnitPrice), 2) AS 'Price'
FROM Products;
```

	Total	Price
1	77	28.87

Figure 13: Sub Query Attempt #1

Note that this example introduced using two new built-in SQL functions upon the data returned. The AVG function, as the abbreviation implies, generates the average for a group of values. Finally we used the ROUND function to display the resulting calculated number with a scale of 2 (i.e. two digits to the right of the decimal point).

However note that the SELECT in Figure 13 returns just one row for the average unit price for all products across all categories – and not just the one having the most products. That's clearly not the answer that we're after.

So let's add the categoryID and a GROUP BY clause so that we now display the product counts and their average unit price per category for all categories, as shown below here in Figure 14.

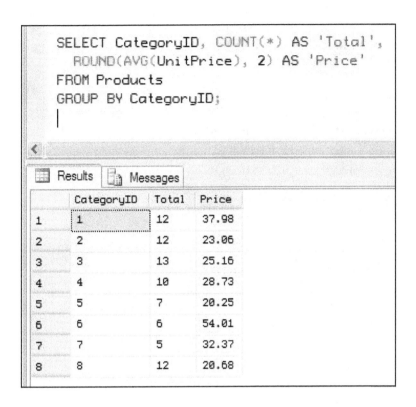

```
SELECT CategoryID, COUNT(*) AS 'Total',
    ROUND(AVG(UnitPrice), 2) AS 'Price'
FROM Products
GROUP BY CategoryID;
```

	CategoryID	Total	Price
1	1	12	37.98
2	2	12	23.06
3	3	13	25.16
4	4	10	28.73
5	5	7	20.25
6	6	6	54.01
7	7	5	32.37
8	8	12	20.68

Figure 14: Sub Query Attempt #2

However note that the SELECT in Figure 14 now returns one row per category for the average pay for all of its products. While in this example it's easy enough to see that the correct answer is categoryID 3 with 13 products each costing an average of $25.16, the database nonetheless had to all the work and display the results for each and every category. Therefore if there had been 1,000 categories, the total amount of internal processing performed would have greatly exceeding what was needed for just the one row of interest. Plus we would have had to manually look at all 1,000 category rows returned to decide which was the correct answer.

We could now cheat as shown here in Figure 15 and now return the same rows but now in descending sorted order – since we know the first row will be the correct one and then simply ignore all of the remaining rows.

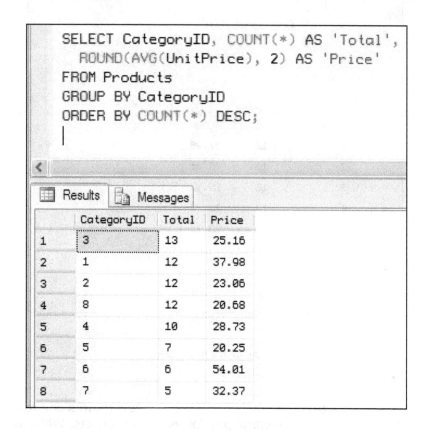

```
SELECT CategoryID, COUNT(*) AS 'Total',
    ROUND(AVG(UnitPrice), 2) AS 'Price'
FROM Products
GROUP BY CategoryID
ORDER BY COUNT(*) DESC;
```

	CategoryID	Total	Price
1	3	13	25.16
2	1	12	37.98
3	2	12	23.06
4	8	12	20.68
5	4	10	28.73
6	5	7	20.25
7	6	6	54.01
8	7	5	32.37

Figure 15: Sub Query Attempt #3

But once again the internal processing expended to process the other non-answer departments (e.g. 999 others) would represent a huge waste of computer resources – and possibly slow the database for everyone else for no extra insights.

The way to solve this is to embed one SELECT command inside another. Think "divide and conquer", which is to say solve bigger problems in smaller, more understandable and thus manageable parts. The SELECT back from Figure 13 labeled "Sub Query Attempt #1" would work (i.e. provide the right answer) if we knew that category 3 was the correct category, and we could thus simply provide a WHERE clause explicitly stating this restriction as shown here in Figure 16. So think of this missing query to provide that now hard coded WHERE clause value as the sub query to nest or embed within this SELECT statement. That's what we'll be developing next, the sub-SELECT to return the category with the most products.

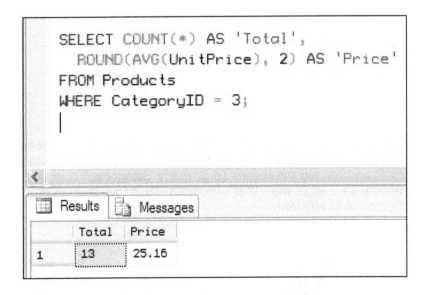

Figure 16: Sub Query Attempt #4

So how do we query the database to find the "TOP N" rows that satisfy our search criteria. SQL Server has a very elegant solution which is simply to use TOP N, because TOP is a valid keyword in the T-SQL language which SQL Server uses. Therefore, we end up with a query like in Figure 17.

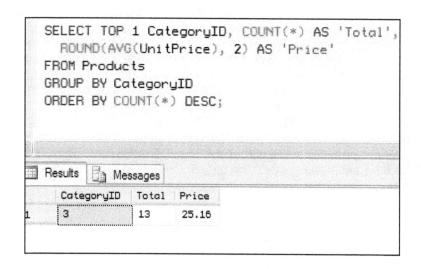

```
SELECT TOP 1 CategoryID, COUNT(*) AS 'Total',
    ROUND(AVG(UnitPrice), 2) AS 'Price'
FROM Products
GROUP BY CategoryID
ORDER BY COUNT(*) DESC;
```

	CategoryID	Total	Price
1	3	13	25.16

Figure 7: TOP N Example

While you might feel that the syntax for this correct answer seems a little overly complex, it nonetheless returns the correct business result and for big databases (e.g. many categories) it does the minimal amount of work that's required. Thus this solution is both effective and efficient.

Don't let the complexity of the syntax bother you – as most SQL commands that truly answer real world business questions will be this complex or more. While there might be some very basic business questions properly answered with trivial SQL like examples in prior chapters, the bulk of genuinely useful SQL commands will require coding efforts more like those in this chapter – and specifically this last section.

CONCLUSION

In this chapter we covered some of the more involved but extremely useful SELECT command constructs and their syntax. The SELECT command varies greatly in complexity from very simple to highly complex. Using just the constructs presented in this chapter one could easily write a SELECT command that's several pages in length to return the correct results for but a single business question. And that query could include multiple SELECT command constructs from this chapter – including joins, outer joins, and sub-SELECT's.

CHAPTER 7: SQL SERVER REPORTING SERVICES

In preparation for SQL Server 2005, Microsoft was working on a new report delivery system called SQL Server Reporting Services (SSRS). It was such a big hit in beta that Microsoft rolled it out prior to the release of SQL Server 2005, code named Yukon, and called it simply SQL Server 2000 Reporting Services. With each new revision of SQL Server, SSRS has been improved. The primary tool for developing reports in SSRS is called Business Intelligence Development Studio (BIDS) and it's basically a Visual Studio development environment tailored just for the pieces of SQL Server related to business intelligence, including SQL Server Reporting Services. In this chapter we'll look briefly at both SSRS and BIDS and how you can use both together to turn your queries into reports.

VIEWING REPORTS

Many organizations now have SQL Server Reporting Services deployed with reports built for a whole host of reasons. Typically these reports are accessed through the web browser. For instance, Figure 1 shows the top level of a SQL Server Reporting Services site. Note that in this example there is a folder, AdventureWorks. SSRS allows you to set up a folder structure just like the Windows file system in order to organize reports together logically.

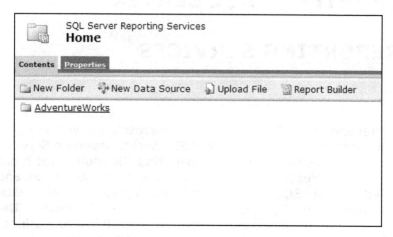

Figure 1: Top Level of SSRS site

Since it is deployed as web application, navigation is intuitive. By clicking on the AdventureWorks folder, we navigate into it and there see its contents (Figure 2). In this case there is one report, Sales By Named Customer. Note also how the navigation information at the top has changed. We see a link going back to Home, the top-level of the site, and the current folder, AdventureWorks is displayed in bold and a larger font.

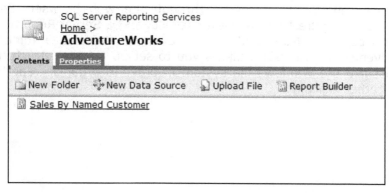

Figure 2: Navigating into AdventureWorks

If we want to view this particular report, we simply click on it. If the report doesn't any parameters, in other words, it doesn't have any user input to filter the results, the report will run immediately. However, Sales By Named Customer does have two parameters: the start and end date to consider sales for this customer report (Figure 3).

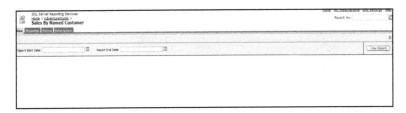

Figure 3: A Parameterized Report

If we specify the dates and then click on the View Report button, SSRS will handle running the report, including going and retrieving the data from the back-end database server. While SQL Server is the most common database platform used to host the data, Reporting Services can connect to any data source, so long as it can establish an ODBC connection. Once the report is rendered, it will be displayed in the browser (Figure 4).

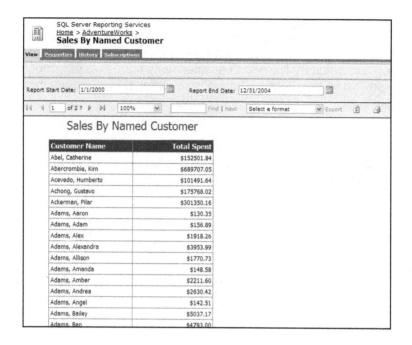

Figure 4: Rendered Report

SQL Server Reporting Services also allows you to take a rendered report and export it to another format. For instance, it's not unusual for a report to be exported into Microsoft Excel for further analysis. This can be done rather easily by selecting the drop down where Select a format... is specified. There are a number of formats, including:

- Adobe Acrobat Reader (.PDF)

- Comma-delimited (.CSV)

- Microsoft Excel Spreadsheet

- Microsoft Word Document

For instance, if I wanted to export the Sales By Named Customer report to Excel, I would simply click the drop down and select Excel. This enables the Export link. Once it is clicked, Reporting Services will send the Excel spreadsheet to the client, which usually results in a file download prompt (Figure 5).

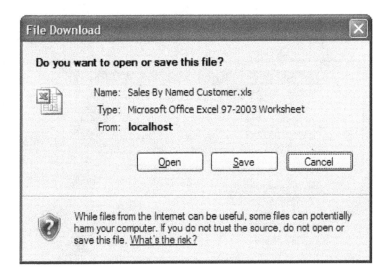

Figure 5: Prompt to open/save extracted data

If you just want to open it, click the Open button and it won't save the spreadsheet locally. You are then free to manipulate the data any way you want to in Microsoft Excel (Figure 6).

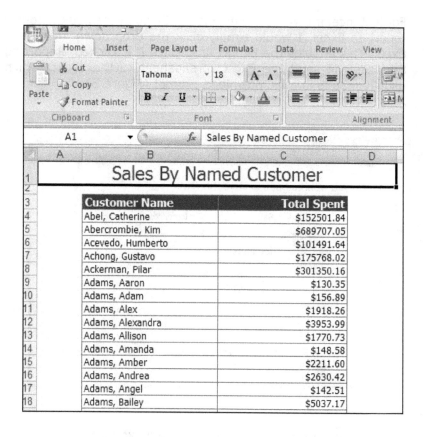

Figure 6: Data Rendered to Excel

INTRODUCING BIDS

I mentioned earlier that Business Intelligence Development Studio is basically a Visual Studio interface with the components for SQL Server's business intelligence features. However, in order to use BIDS for building reports, you don't have to be a developer. BIDS is plenty powerful with the GUI tools.

You'll find BIDS underneath either the SQL Server 2005 or SQL Server 2008 folder (Figure 7), depending on which version of the client tools you have installed. If you're a developer and already have Visual Studio installed, since BIDS is really just the Visual Studio Interactive Development Environment (IDE), you can start Reporting Services project by going into Visual Studio.

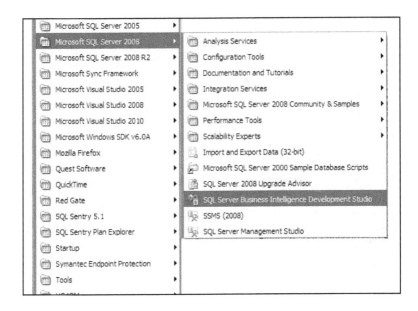

Figure 7: BIDS location

BUILDING A REPORT

If you're not familiar with Visual Studio, you probably aren't familiar with BIDS. In Microsoft development speak, we usually talk about building projects and solutions. And so if we want to build reports to deploy to SQL Server Reporting Services, we'll need to create a new project of the appropriate type. To start a new project, go to the menu and select File > New > Project. BIDS will bring up a dialog window where you can select the type of project you want to work on (Figure 8).

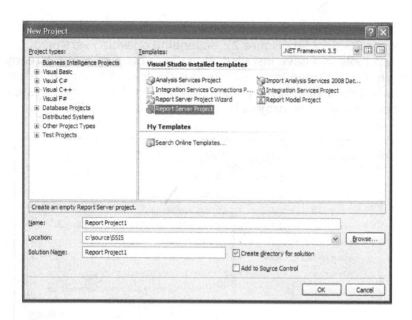

Figure 8: Choose a Project in BIDS

You'll want to make sure in the left hand pane you select Business Intelligence Projects and in the right hand pane you select one of the Report Server Project choices. We'll use the Report Server Project Wizard choice to quick-start a project so we can quickly build and deploy a report. Make sure you give your project a name and you can choose to store your project files at a different path than the default (the example I used is set to a non-default path because I do a lot of work in SQL Server Integration Services).

The first dialog window to come up is one asking you to tell the project where your data is, as is shown in Figure 9.

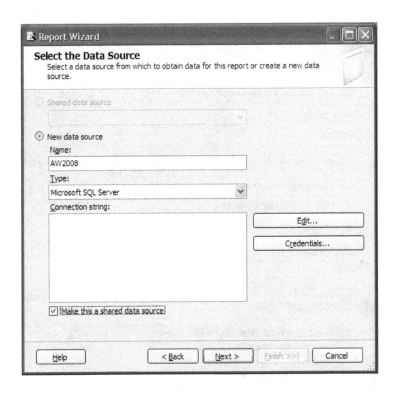

Figure 9: Define the Data Source

You'll want to give your data source a name that will help you remember what it is. For instance, I know I'm going to build a report against a sample database known as AdventureWorks2008, so I'll name the data source AW2008. If you're connecting to a SQL Server, you'll need to build a connection string. This is easy to do. Just click the Edit button. BIDS will pop up a dialog window to help define the data connection, as in figure 10.

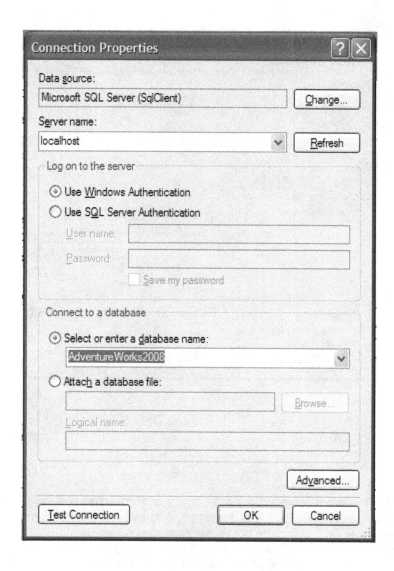

Figure 10: Connection dialog window

You'll need to specify the SQL Server and the database, just like in chapter 2. If need be, you can test your connection before going any further. Once you've defined your connection, BIDS will take you back to the previous window and you'll see the connection string text box populated. If you don't know any of that means, don't worry, it's not a big deal at this time. A DBA can always assist and even make changes to a data source, even after it is deployed to Reporting Services. And once you're back, if you know that others may want to use this same data source or if you're eventually going to build several reports all connecting to the same database, click the checkbox to make it a shared data source.

The next dialog window is where you'll specify the query the report will be built around. If you need the GUI tools to build the query, click on the Query builder button (Figure 11). Since I had already built a query, I just pasted it into the text box and clicked next. I'm building a report to tell me when all employees were hired.

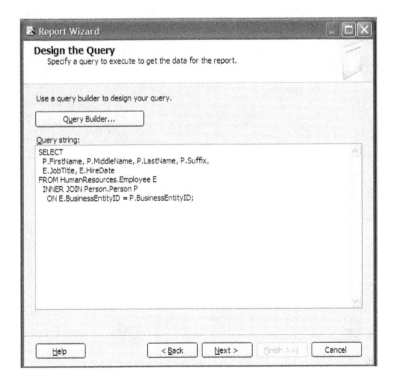

Figure 11: Define the Query

Now that the data connection and the query is defined, the wizard will ask you if you want the report to display in a tabular or matrix format. Then the wizard will ask how you want to arrange the data in the report. Do you want to group based on a certain column? Do you want each page separate by other columns? Since I have a very basic report, all of my columns are going into the detail section, as shown in figure 12.

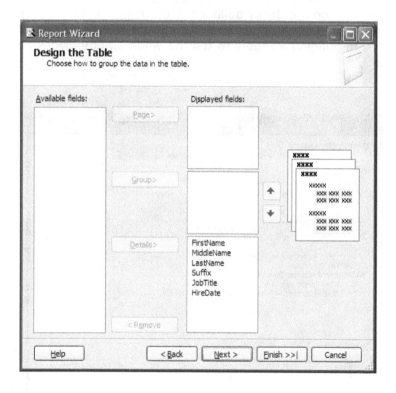

Figure 12 How to Display the Data

You then have the option of selecting how the report might look (BIDS has a handful of default templates). And then we get to a window where you will probably need to ask beforehand about. This page asks where the Reporting Services server is and what folder to deploy to. Likely your DBA will know this if you don't already have the information. I have a SSRS install locally, so I'll specify that for my Reporting Services report server and I'll make sure that I'm putting the report in the AdventureWorks folder, like in figure 13.

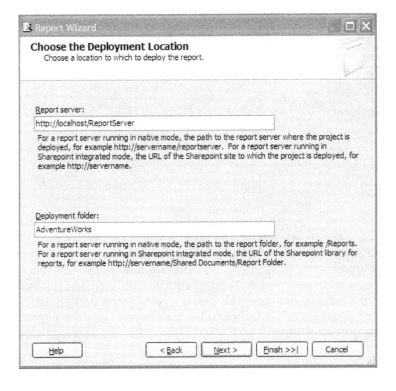

Figure 13: Deployment Location

The final screen allows you to name your report. I'm simply going to name it All Employees. Then click Finish to allow the wizard finish up creating the basic report.

GETTING READY TO DEPLOY

Once the wizard is done building the basic report, you should see the report defined like in Figure 14.

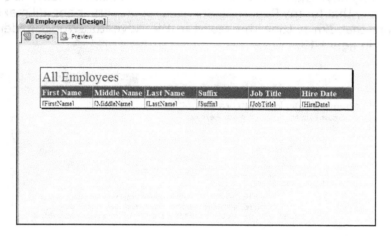

Figure 14: Report Design

If you want to see how it should look once it is deployed, click on the Preview tab. The first time you preview the report, or anytime you make changes, don't be surprised if BIDS tells you in a window along the lower bottom that it is saving and/or building the project. That's normal. Now, if you were building a report which required parameters to be configured, you'd be prompted once you clicked on the tab. In Figure 15, we see a preview of the rendered report.

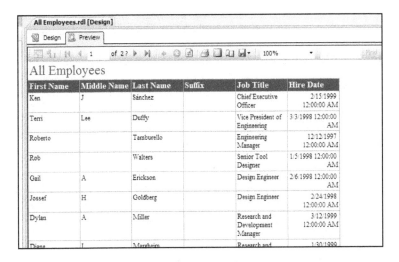

Figure 15: Report Preview

If the preview looks good, you'll want to deploy the report. In the case of the report that was just built, the spacing and column widths are wrong and need to be adjusted first. This can be done by going back to the Design tab and making the appropriate changes with the GUI tools.

In addition to changing the column widths, I'm also going to fix the display for Hire Date. Since I'm interested in when a person was hired and the 12:00:00 AM is meaningless, I want to get rid of the time. This is showing up because the HireDate column in SQL Server is of datetime, meaning it has to have both. But we don't have to display both.

To fix this, I simply double-click on [HireDate] so it highlights (not the header cell, but the one below it). Then if I look in the right hand pane, there should be properties. If you don't see the properties, you can make them visible by going to View > Properties Windows.

If I scroll down, I'll see a choice called Format under Number. If I click on it, I get a drop down which allows me to specify an expression by clicking on <Expression...> (Figure 16).

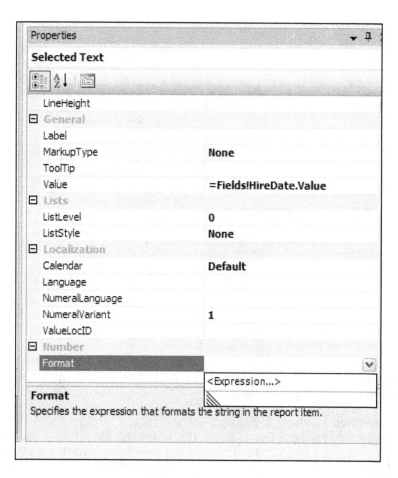

Properties	▾ 〓
Selected Text	

LineHeight	
⊟ General	
Label	
MarkupType	**None**
ToolTip	
Value	**=Fields!HireDate.Value**
⊟ Lists	
ListLevel	0
ListStyle	**None**
⊟ Localization	
Calendar	**Default**
Language	
NumeralLanguage	
NumeralVariant	1
ValueLocID	
⊟ Number	
Format	⌄

<Expression...>

Format
Specifies the expression that formats the string in the report item.

Figure 16: Properties

This will bring up a dialog window where I can specify the format. I know there is function under Common Functions > Date & Time which allows me to format the date called FormatDateTime. If I double-click on it, it'll move it up to the top text box and then give me Intellisense™ hints as to how to finish completing that function. The first parameter is whatever is being modified. I know I need to modify a data field (another name for a column) and specifically the HireDate field. I should find that under Fields (Dataset1) and once I do, I can double-click on HireDate to have it inserted properly. Then I type a comma to indicate I want to specify the second parameter, which is how the data is being formatted. This is where you may need a bit of help from a developer or you may need to look on MSDN (http://msdn.microsoft.com) every so often. However, when I first looked at FormatDateTime, it told me that there was a format called DateFormat.ShortDate. That happens to give me just the date. So I'll type that in, close the parentheses and click OK (Figure 17). If the function is set up correctly, you shouldn't get an error.

Figure 17: Format Date

Now it is possible to fix this in the data query by using the CONVERT() function. However, if we haven't done so, BIDS gives us powerful options to getting the data to look exactly as we want it to.

Once you get to the point where you're satisfied with the look of the report, it's time to deploy it. You can do this by going back up to the menu bar and selecting Build > Deploy *(Project Name)*.

BIDS will go through building and then deploying your report(s) as specified. If in the process of deploying a report you get a warning indicating you can't deploy a shared data source, that's usually okay. You have to specify a data source for your reports to use and if you're adding reports, likely a shared data source already exists on the SSRS site for the reports you're building. But any other warnings and definitely any errors you should investigate. Usually they are something simple to resolve.

If the report deployed successfully, we should find it underneath the AdventureWorks folder and sure enough we do (Figure 18). Also note that the report has a !NEW beside it to get our attention.

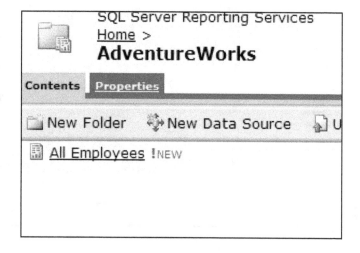

Figure 18: Deployed Report

If we click on the report we should see it render similar to how it displayed under preview in BIDS. And sure enough, it did, complete with the proper date formatting (Figure 19).

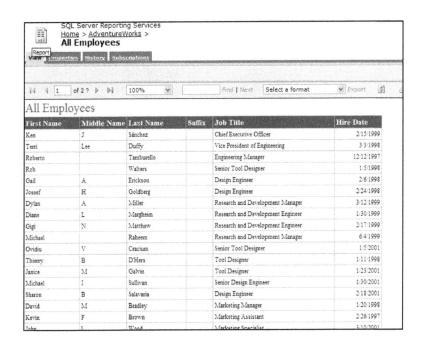

Figure 19: Our Report Displayed!

CONCLUSION

In this chapter we first covered what SQL Server Reporting Services is, which is Microsoft's packaged reporting solution for displaying data from any source to which an ODBC connection can be made. SSRS is a web application, meaning we can connect with a web browser and get our reports that way.

CHAPTER 8: TOAD

This chapter will cover the same topics as the last, but this time on Quest Software's TOAD for SQL Server (often just called TOAD) rather than any of the Microsoft provided tools. While the Microsoft client tools come with the SQL Server media, some find that a third party tool works better for them. TOAD has been around for well over a decade for various database platforms (like Oracle) and is on version 5.X for SQL Server. Since TOAD was the only real good tool for a long time, many shops and people standardized on it on these other platforms and they are able to transfer their knowledge to its use on SQL Server. So even though the Microsoft tools are provided with the server product, they have long history and investment in TOAD – and thus cannot switch. As such, there are some million people worldwide using TOAD. Therefore we have decided to include a chapter on TOAD.

Note – Quest Software offers TOAD for SQL Sever as both a freeware available on www.toadsoft.com and as a pay-for commercial product. The commercial version offers numerous additional features and several bundles for various roles – such as analyst, developer and DBA.

INSTALL

TOAD freeware and commercial are both regular Windows programs that are installed like any other – i.e. via an executable (i.e. EXE) file or Microsoft installer (i.e. MSI) file, depending on the TOAD version. Depending on your Windows Vista and Windows 7.0 User Access Control (i.e. UAC) settings, you may have perform the install using a user in the administrators group.

The TOAD freeware times out every sixty days and requires that no more than five people per company use it. When the freeware expires, you simply download a zip file with an updated exe and unzip that file in your TOAD install directory. You do not have to get the full installer and perform a complete install each time.

CONNECTING

In order to work with any database you must first create or establish a connection – often referred to as "*logging on*" to the database (refer back to Chapter 3). For that you simply choose from the TOAD main menu File -> New -> Connection or click on the plug with a star burst icon in the Connection Manager window, both of which launch the database login screen shown here in Figure 1.

Figure 1: Creating a Connection

You simply provide the requisite connection information: server name, method of authentication and login with password if you're using SQL Server-based authentication (refer back to Chapter 2).

Once a database connection has been defined and made, TOAD will then automatically open whatever screen you've defined in its plethora of options – by default it will open an occurrence of the "*Editor*".

BROWSING

One of the most basic and useful tasks in working with any database is to investigate or "*snoop around*" to see what's available (i.e. tables, views, etc). Of course if you already know the database or have at least worked with it some, you may do less browsing. But when you first start working with a new database, browsing may well be the chief activity that you perform.

TOAD has an "Object Explorer" window which makes all database browsing trivially easy. You launch it either via the main menu View -> Object Explorer or by pressing the F8 key. The Object Explorer expands to show you all the database object types available to you as shown in Figure 2.

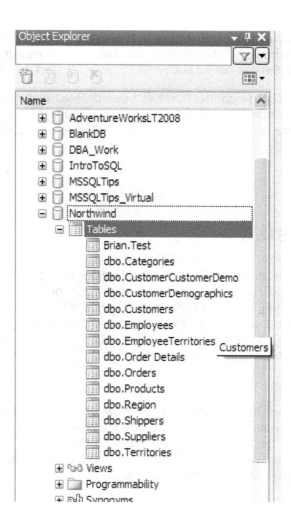

Figure 2: Object Explorer

While TOAD calls this tree-view the *"Object Explorer"*, you may hear people refer to it as either the database explorer or database browser. But by whatever name you call it, it provides our *"road map"* to the database. You will therefore browse the database's meta-data or data dictionary using this facility.

Once you single click on or select a named object on the right hand side, such as the Products table, TOAD will display object details within Object Explorer as shown in Figure 3.

Figure 3: Table Details

Note that as is typical in a Windows application, if you right-click on an object, you'll get a whole lot more options. For instance, if you right-click on Products you can choose to generate a Creation Script for that table (Figure 4).

Figure 4: Choosing to Generate Creation Script

You can also choose to send an object to a new window, which will give you several tabs relevant to the given object. For instance, in Figure 5 the Products table has been sent to a new window and the data tab has selected to display the contents of the table.

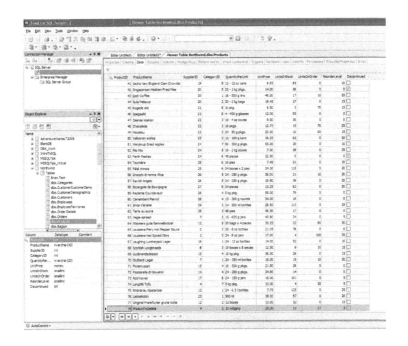

Figure 5: Data Sub-Tab

The bottom navigator icons of plus (i.e. +) and minus (i.e. -) signs allow you to add and/or delete rows respectively. However, you must first toggle the table as not Read Only, which is the default. To do this, you will need to click on the down arrow next to the red circle (indicating "stop" and you can't make changes) and then uncheck the Read Only property. As the ProductToDelete row is highlighted in Figure 5, pressing the minus sign after changing out of Read Only mode will result in that row being deleted from the data grid (see Figure 6). You will likely be prompted to confirm the delete (unless you've told TOAD never to warn you again), and after you confirm the delete will be performed. The changes will be made to the database and visible to all other users if confirmed, and will revert to the original data if rejected.

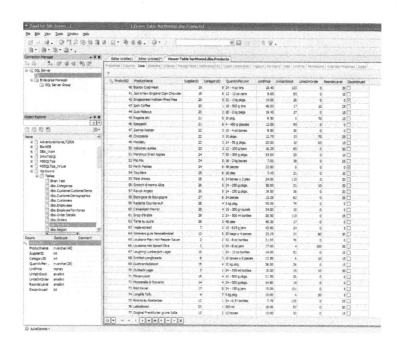

Figure 6: Deleting Rows

Of course since most tables have far more rows than once can effectively view and work with, TOAD provides a simple filter mechanism to restrict the rows displayed – the funnel toolbar icon. When the funnel is gray, no filters are in force. When it appears to have bubbles above the funnel, then there are filters in force restricting the data rows returned. Pressing the funnel launches the sort/filter screen shown here in Figure 7 – think of this as simply a WHERE clause appended to a SELECT upon the table.

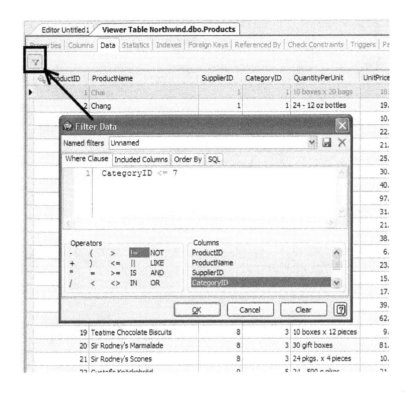

Figure 7: Filtering the Data

Thus to display only the rows for products with a CategoryID of less than or equal to 7, we simply add the SQL code for that restriction. Often when viewing the table data, you'll want to sort the results to make them easier to scan, comprehend and digest. By pressing the funnel toolbar icon a pop-up window will permit you to specify one or more column to sort upon as shown here in Figure 8. Once you've selected the sort columns, note how the funnel icon now also includes a blue halo or crown.

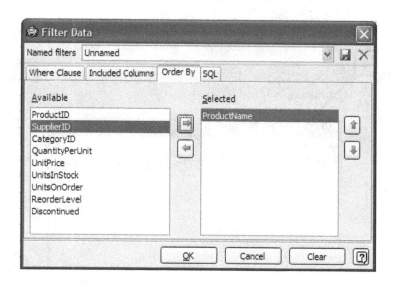

Figure 8: Sorting the Data

Once you've found the data that you're after, it's time to do something with it. In many cases you'll simply want to get a copy to work with in some other tool. For example to export this data into a Microsoft Excel spreadsheet, you now simply mouse onto the data grid, press the right hand mouse, and then choose Quick Export > Excel Instance > Excel Instance.

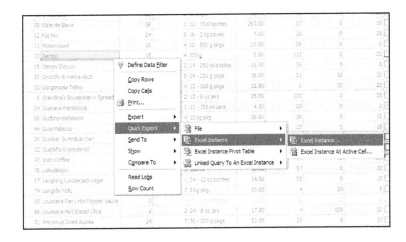

Figure 9: Exporting the Data

TOAD will open an Excel spreadsheet as shown in Figure 10. And now you can use all the tools of Excel to manipulate the data..

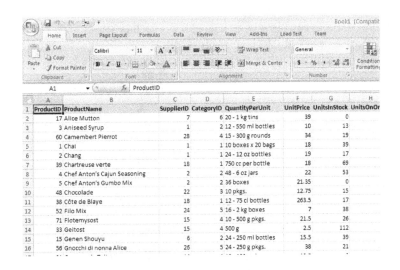

Figure 10: Export Data Wizard

QUERYING

When you first connect to a database, TOAD will automatically open a SQL Editor for that connection as shown here in Figure 11.

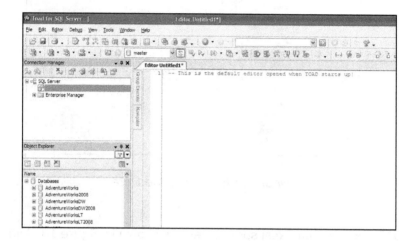

Figure 11: SQL Worksheet

This SQL Editor is simply a SQL editing facility much like Windows Notepad – except that it understands the SQL language (i.e. performs syntax highlighting). Once you type some SQL code the Window will activate additional toolbar icons as shown here Figure 12.

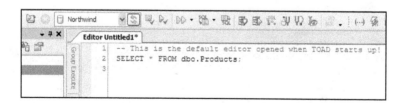

Figure 12: Query Entered

The first toolbar icon, the green triangle with the sheet of paper, represents the "*Execute*" option.

The "*Execute*" toolbar icon and its F5 keyboard shortcut simply mean to run the command and display the results in a data grid exactly like when the Object Explorer sent the table to a new window in the prior section. Thus the results (i.e. data grid) will appear as shown here in Figure 13.

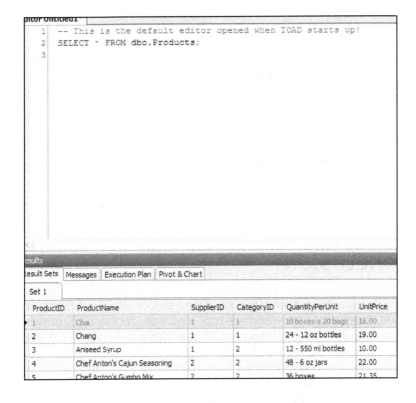

Figure 13: Execute

Note that the newly added "Result Sets" section appears very similar to the "Object Explorer's *Data*" right hand side tab back in Figure 5 – minus most of the toolbar icons, sort button, filter box and actions drop-down. However some of those actions (e.g. export data) are available via the right hand menu as shown in Figure 14. That's why the "Object Explorer" was covered first – because you need to know about the database objects to work with them, and the "Execute" works the same as the "Data" right hand side tab.

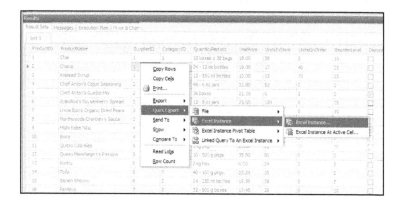

Figure 14: Data Grid Right-Hand-Menu

CONCLUSION

In this chapter we covered the very basics of Quest Software's TOAD graphical user interface tool – namely connecting, browsing and querying the database. These activities will most likely represent 80% or more of what most people do on a regular basis. And with this basic introductory knowledge, any user should be able to investigate further and eventually master TOAD. Both the TOAD freeware and commercial versions are great assets when working with any SQL Server database – as it makes users much more productive. It lets you concentrate on what you need to do rather than how to do it.

CHAPTER 9: MICROSOFT OFFICE

Let's face it – for corporate desktops Microsoft Office has a near monopoly. Most workers, from information systems geek's to frontline business users, have some version of Microsoft Office on their PC. And as was shown in previous chapters, many people will use database tools like SQL Server Management Studio and TOAD to export the data they need into other tools, such as Microsoft Excel or Access. Here we'll learn how to utilize your SQL Server database directly from within your Microsoft Office tools. Because some of you will be able to skip the interim tool and export once you see how to do it from within Microsoft Office.

MS EXCEL

Business people have become experts or "*gurus*" on Microsoft Excel. So much so that many business analysts have become essentially Excel application developers and/or programmers. There are even professional certifications from Microsoft on Excel.

Some business people use their information system people simply to find and export their SQL Server data for them, which they then perform their magic on using Excel. But Excel can directly access your SQL Server database and it's not that hard to do.

Let's see how we'd get our Product table data into a spreadsheet for further work within Microsoft Excel 2007. You start by clicking on the Data tab on the ribbon then From Other Sources > From SQL Server, as shown in Figure 1.

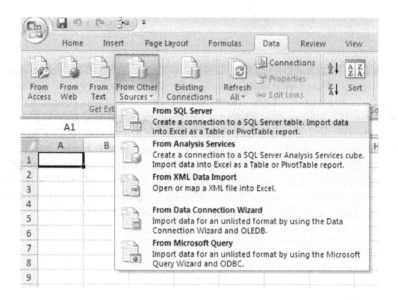

Figure 1: Excel Database Query

This will launch the Data Connection Wizard as shown below in Figure 2 where you specify what SQL Server to use for your database connection and how you will authenticate (refer back to Chapter 2 on how to set this up).

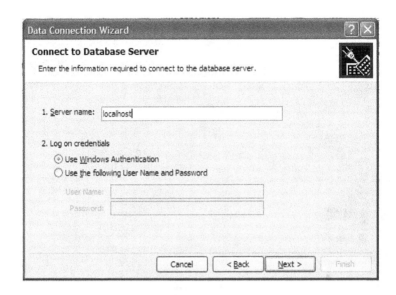

Figure 2: Connect to SQL Server

When you click Next, Excel will attempt to connect to SQL Server and then present you with the next screen, which will allow you to select what tables you want to query data from. Do note that when the interface says tables, it means tables and views in "SQL Server speak." You will likely need to change the database to get to the proper table. This is shown in Figure 3.

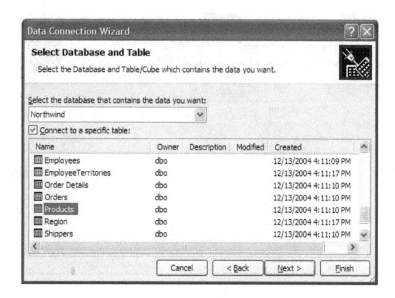

Figure 3: Select Table

Once you've selected the table to use in the database, you'll then see a final screen in the Data Connection Wizard to specify the name of the connection and to provide some information about it as you save it, as shown in Figure 4.

Figure 4: Saving the SQL Server Connection

Once the Data Connection Wizard is finished, Excel will then prompt you on how you want to display the data (Figure 5).

Figure 5: How to Display Data

Once you've specified how you want the data displayed, Excel then imports the data and displays it as you specified. Figure 6 shows the default, where the data was placed into the existing worksheet.

Figure 6: Data Pulled into Excel

If you want to pull in a query that's more complex than just returning everything from a single table, then you'll need to use the Microsoft Query Wizard. To bring it up, click on the Data table and then click on From Other Sources on the ribbon and then From Microsoft Query. It should bring up an interface like in Figure 7.

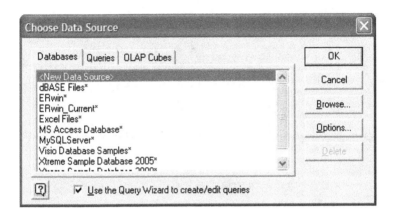

Figure 7: Microsoft Query Wizard

You'll want to create a <New Data Source> and click OK. This will bring up a dialog box where you'll need to specify the name of this connection as well as what driver to use. You'll want to select SQL Server or the appropriate SQL Server Native Client (if installed) if you're connecting to a SQL Server 2005 server (the client will be 9.0) or SQL Server 2008 server (the client will be 10.0). If you aren't sure, the SQL Server driver should work fine. Then you'll be ready to click the Connect button, like in Figure 8.

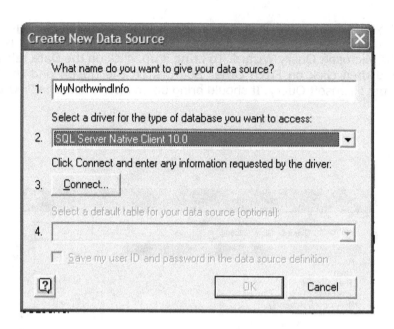

Figure 8: Defining New Connection

You'll need to specify what SQL Server to connect to and what kind of authentication to use. If you are connecting using your Windows account, click the Use Trusted Connection checkbox. If you're using a SQL Server login specify the correct login ID and password (your DBA should be able to provide the right credentials). And to complete the configuration, typically you'll leave the SPN blank unless specified by your DBA. Also, if you need to specify the database, click on the Options button, which will expand the dialog box and let you select the database you want to use from a drop down (Figure 9).

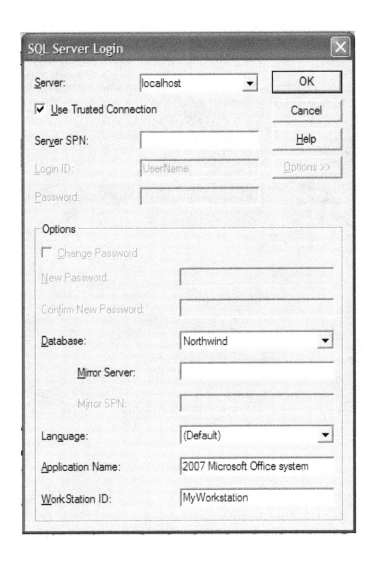

Figure 9: Define Server Connection

Once that is all configured, click OK and you'll be taken back to the Create Data Source dialog box and you'll be prompted if you want to use a default table (don't select one at this time). Click OK to return to Choose Data Source. This actually creates an

ODBC Data Source for use (meaning you can use it by other applications, too). Click on the Data Source you want to use and then click the OK button. This should bring up the Query Wizard where you can choose how to put your query together.

Select the columns you want, and click the arrows to move them into the query (right arrow) or out of the query (left arrow) like in Figure 10. The Query Wizard is pretty smart and if there are foreign keys in place, it'll figure out the JOIN's if you select multiple tables.

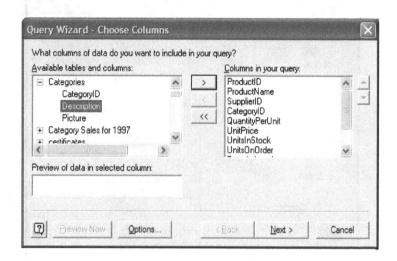

Figure 10: Choosing Columns

You'll get additional screens to choose how to filter and how to sort your data. Once all of those choices are made, you'll have the option of previewing the query in Microsoft Query or returning straight to Excel. If you preview the Query in Microsoft Query, you can tweak the query as necessary. This is often useful if Excel can't figure out how certain tables relate. Once you're done working with the query and feel it is ready, you'll be prompted where to insert the data in Excel. The query result will then be inserted into Excel as you've specified (Figure 11). And if you compare Figures 6 and 11, you'll see Figure 11 has the Category Name, because we pulled in the Categories table, too.

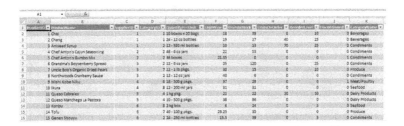

Figure 11: Custom Query in Excel

MS ACCESS

For those lucky enough to have Microsoft Office Professional, you already have a top notch database tool that you can use – MS Access. Plus you can operate in one of two modes: work on the actual data in the SQL Server database or make a local Access database copy to work with.

As with the prior section, you'll first need to have a SQL Server ODBC data source (often called a DSN for Data Source Name) defined on your machine (refer back to Chapter 2 on how to set this up).

You'll then need to click on the Office Button within Microsoft Access and then click Open. That will launch the typical Windows application file open screen. On that screen choose a file type of ODBC Databases, which is the last choice on the drop-down box. You'll then see pop-up screens similar to what you saw back in Chapter 2. Select the appropriate DSN and click OK.

Access will now display its database link definition screen as shown here in Figure 12. Here you can select all the SQL Server tables and/or views that you want to be able to work with from within Access.

Figure 12: Table Link Selection

When you press the "*OK*" button be prepared to wait. You'll see a progress bar of sorts as Access reaches out to SQL Server to both find and understand the database objects that you've selected. Once that process completes you'll see the typical Access database work options as shown here in Figure 13.

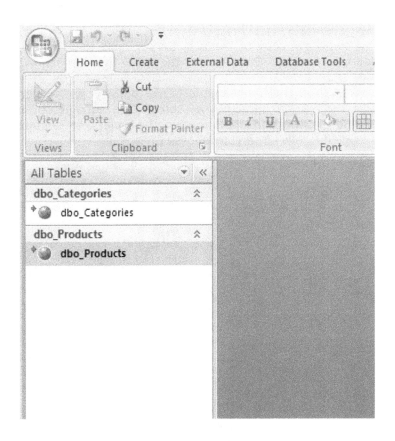

Figure 13: Access Links to SQL Server

You'll notice the little arrow pointing to a globe icon next to each of the tables listed. This indicates that these are external tables with links to be worked upon via Access. So the SQL Server tables and their data are still on the SQL Server database server and not copied onto your PC.

You now can use any of Microsoft Access' tools and techniques to work with your data. However in this case it will simply be sending the SQL over to SQL Server and fetching back the resulting rows. The local Access database files (i.e. ODBC.MDB) will only contain the meta-data and pointers to the SQL Server database – and thus will be very small.

To make a local copy of the SQL Server table you will need to click on the External Data tab and then click the More icon where it says Import data and choose an ODBC Database as shown in Figure 14. You then choose the ODBC data source, choose to import the source data into a table in the current database, provide the connection info and select the table(s) to be imported (i.e. copied locally) into your Access Database.

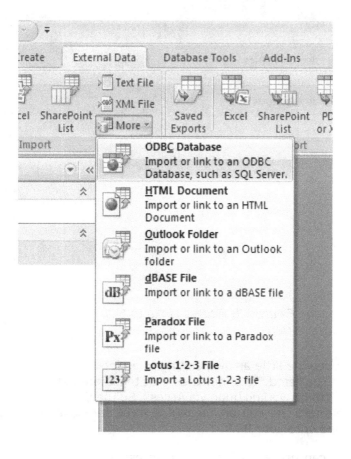

Figure 14: Importing Tables

When you're successfully completed the table import you'll now see a local copy of that table in your object list with a table icon (i.e. grid) next to it as shown in Figure 15.

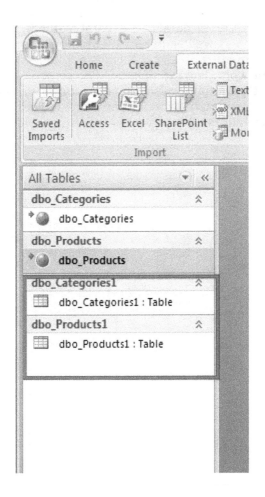

Figure 15: Local Tables in the Access DB

Two items to note. First, the bigger the table you import the longer it will take and the more network traffic it will cause. Second, your local hard drive better have sufficient room to host all the data that SQL Server returns.

CONCLUSION

In this chapter we covered using your existing Microsoft Office tools to directly work with your SQL Server database. Excel can link into your SQL Server data via a several methods. Access can link to your tables as well as import them into local copies. Plus Access offers numerous other capabilities and tools which might assist with your work. For example building screens and reports in Access is pretty straightforward and easy. So why attempt that work in some other database tool when you have perfectly good tools already on your PC that you know and use everyday already.

CHAPTER 10: DATABASE

SANDBOX

Sometimes the quickest and best way to learn any new technology is to create a sandbox or playground type environment where you can try your new skills without worrying about impacting other people. Microsoft SQL Server comes in a mix of editions that range from free to ones only a large business can afford.

SQL Server Express is a free edition which has most of the features of SQL Server, but it's missing the SQL Server Agent, which can schedule jobs, as well as the nice client tools to connect and write SQL queries with. However, there is a free edition of the SQL Server Management Studio (SSMS), aptly called SQL Server Management Studio Express, which has most of the features of SSMS.

Editions of SQL Server you must pay for but can run on a "production" server include Web Edition, Standard Edition, Enterprise Edition, and Datacenter Edition. Standard Edition and Enterprise Edition are typically seen in use for businesses while Datacenter Edition is used for very large SQL Server requirements.

There is one other edition of SQL Server that's available for $50. It's called Developer Edition and has all the features of Enterprise Edition, but it can be installed on just about every supported Operating System Microsoft supports, including Windows XP SP3, Windows Vista, and Windows 7. The one catch with it is it cannot be used in "production." If you want to develop with it, that's perfectly fine.

The Express Edition is a very simple to install, easy to use and easy to manage version of the SQL Server database. It has most of the features of the standard edition, so it makes for an excellent learning arena. It does have some database size (10 GB for each database) and computer resource limits (1 GB RAM and 1 CPU) – but for basic SQL Server experimentation and learning these limits should not be an issue. Plus the Express Edition is totally free, there are no options or requirements for any kind of purchase. If you can, look to get the latest version your operating system supports. SQL Server Express is designed to be as lightweight as possible and intentionally limits its resources as best as possible. As of this writing, the most recent version was SQL Server 2008 R2 Express Edition.

INSTALLATION

There are several downloads available depending on what features you want and whether your system is 32-bit or 64-bit. You should find the latest versions of the installation at http://www.microsoft.com/express/database/. If you already have client tools from a SQL Server installation, then likely you only need the database engine. That is what is shown here in this chapter.

The Microsoft SQL Server Express Edition installer is a normal Windows application and it varies in size depending on version and the features you want to install. As with other windows installers you merely launch it and answer some fairly basic questions. That's it.

The SQL Server Express installer will display about several dialog windows as part of the overall install process. The first screen of note allows is what initially comes up when you run the installation package as shown here in Figure 1. Unless you know you have an existing, older version of SQL Server Express installed on your computer, you'll want to select the top option, to install a new version.

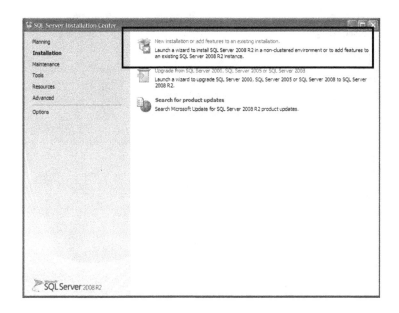

Figure 1: Install Choices Screen

The second installer screen of significance is the one where you'll specify the features, as in Figure 2. If you just want the bare bones to learn how to work with the SQL language and manipulating data, you'll only need the Database Engine Services. The replication piece is necessary if you're synchronizing data with another server by the use of replication technology (and with a sandbox you likely won't). The SQL Client Connectivity SDK is if you're trying to write software using the client connection extensions, which again isn't necessary if you're just looking for a sandbox to work with.

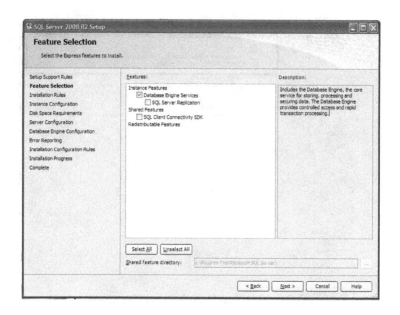

Figure 2: Feature Selection

After that, you'll be prompted for the instance name of the database. If you remember from chapter 2, SQL Server is built so you can install multiple versions of the database engine on the same system. If this is the first engine you're installing, it's perfectly okay to install it as a default engine. That means you'll refer to it as your computer's name. In my case I have other instances, so I'll call mine SQL2008R2, as in figure 3. So when I try to connect I will refer to my instance as MyComputerName\SQL2008R2.

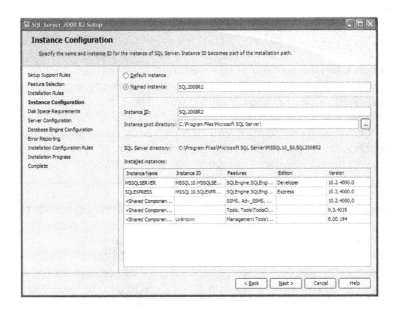

Figure 3: Select Instance Name

You'll then be prompted as to what user account you want your database engine to run under (Figure 4).

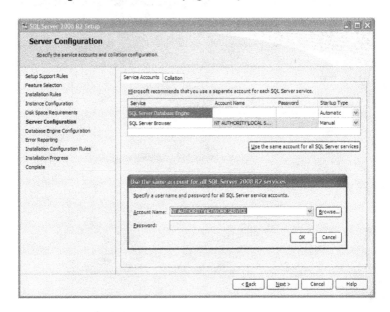

Figure 4: Choose Service Account

It is perfectly okay to run everything under the same account by clicking the Use the same account for all SQL Server services. If you don't have a particular user account in mind, you can hit the drop down and select from two accounts, one corresponding to Network Service and the other System. The System account has administrator level rights on your system and SQL Server does not need this. Therefore, if you don't already have an account to use, choose Network Service. You shouldn't specify your own account, because whenever your password changes you'll have to remember to change it for SQL Server too.

You will then be prompted to determine what sort of authentication will be permitted by your SQL Server and who has administrative rights. By default, the setup selects Windows authentication mode. This means you have to be a Windows or domain user that has been granted rights to connect to the SQL Server. If you want to play around with SQL Server based logins (refer back to chapter 2), then specify Mixed Mode. But if you do so, ensure that you specify a strong password (Figure 5).

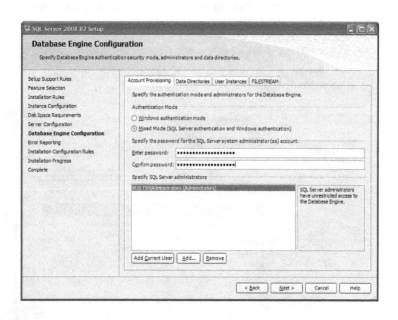

Figure 5: Choose Authentication

In addition, you can specify who has administrative rights and by default your user account will be listed. I've removed mine and put administrators because I use multiple accounts on my system, but unless there is a great reason to change this, leaving your user account is fine.

If you look closely, you'll see other tables labeled Data Directories, User Instances, and FILESTREAM. Data Directories allow you to specify where the SQL Server data files will go. Unless you have a specific reason to need to change this, the defaults are fine. User Instances determines whether when a non-admin user connects to the SQL Server, if SQL Server spawns a separate process for that user. If you want SQL Server Express to run in a traditional mode, uncheck the box. If you're not sure, it's okay to leave it as is. Finally, FILESTREAM is an advanced topic and you don't need to install it at this time.

The next window is if you want your error reports to go back automatically to Microsoft. This should be sent anonymously whenever you have a network connection. I typically leave it unchecked, but it's your choice. And finally, when you click Next from that screen, the installation begins. This may take a bit, especially on older systems, as the SQL Server install has quite a few tasks to do.

UTILITIES

Once the SQL Server Express Edition installer has completed, you'll find the following new application shortcuts under the Start menu -> Programs as shown here in Figure 6.

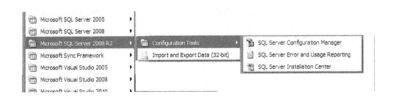

Figure 6: SQL Server Express Programs

You may have other tools depending on which version of the installation you chose. One tool you should be familiar with is the SQL Server Configuration Manager under the Configuration Tools folder. It's what you can use to configure your SQL Server Express instance with respect to start up, service account, and whether or not it listens on the network (by default it only listens on your computer).

Note that by default the SQL Server Express Edition database is setup to automatically start a windows boot. So your database will be available every time you start your PC as shown here in Figure 7 (the SQL Server Configuration Manager). You might want to change the SQL Server service [here, the one marked SQL Server (SQL2008R2) is the instance that was just installed] to not start automatically by setting it to Manual to keep your PC boot time reasonable. You can always start the database when needed by bringing up SQL Server Configuration Manager and manually starting it from the interface.

Name	State	Start Mode
SQL Server Integration Services 10.0	Stopped	Manual
SQL Server (SQL2008R2)	Running	Manual
SQL Server (SQLEXPRESS)	Stopped	Manual
SQL Full-text Filter Daemon Launcher (MSSQL...	Stopped	Manual
SQL Server (MSSQLSERVER)	Stopped	Manual

Figure 7: SQL Server Configuration Manager

SSMS EXPRESS

If you don't already have access to the SQL Server client tools, which includes SQL Server Management Studio and you don't want to use TOAD or another tool, there is a free download from Microsoft called SQL Server Management Studio Express. It was written for those who have SQL Server Express databases to manage but don't have the full set of client tools. If you selected the installer that had the management tools, this should have been included. However, if you didn't get that version of the installer, you can always go back to the link mentioned at the beginning of the chapter and download just SSMS Express. It has most of the features of SQL Server Management Studio and should serve for anything you want to do in your sandbox.

CONCLUSION

In this chapter we covered how to create a SQL Server sandbox or playground for you to experiment with and not risk production data or interfering with other peoples' work. The SQL Server Express Edition is totally free, offers all the database features of significance, and is fairly lightweight in terms of install space and computer resources consumed. Thus by working with your very own local SQL Server database you can learn more and faster – and all with no worries.

AUTHOR BIO'S

Bert Scalzo is a Database Expert for Quest Software and a member of the TOAD dev team. He has worked with Oracle databases for well over two decades. Mr. Scalzo's work history includes time at both Oracle Education and Oracle Consulting. He holds several Oracle Masters certifications and an extensive academic background - including a BS, MS and PhD in Computer Science, an MBA, plus insurance industry designations. Mr. Scalzo is also an Oracle ACE.

Mr. Scalzo is accomplished speaker and has presented at numerous Oracle conferences and user groups - including OOW, ODTUG, IOUG, OAUG, RMOUG and many others. His key areas of DBA interest are Data Modeling, Database Benchmarking, Database Tuning & Optimization, "Star Schema" Data Warehouses, Linux and VMware.

Mr. Scalzo has written numerous articles, papers and blogs - including for the Oracle Technology Network (OTN), Oracle Magazine, Oracle Informant, PC Week (eWeek), Dell Power Solutions Magazine, The LINUX Journal, LINUX.com, Oracle FAQ, Ask Toad and Toad World.

Mr. Scalzo has also written numerous books:

- Oracle DBA Guide to Data Warehousing and Star Schemas

- TOAD Handbook (1st Ed.)

- TOAD Handbook (2nd Ed.)

- TOAD Pocket Reference (2nd Ed.)

- Database Benchmarking: Practical Methods for Oracle & SQL Server

- Advanced Oracle Utilities: The Definitive Reference

- Oracle on VMware: Expert Tips for Database Virtualization

- Introduction to Oracle: Basic Skills for Any Oracle User

- Introduction to SQL Server: Basic Skills for Any SQL Server User

K. Brian Kelley is a SQL Server author, columnist, and Microsoft MVP focusing primarily on SQL Server security. He is a contributing author for How to Cheat at Securing SQL Server 2005 (Syngress) and Professional SQL Server 2008 Administration (Wrox). Brian currently serves as a database administrator / architect for AgFirst Farm Credit Bank where he can concentrate on his passion: SQL Server. He previously was a systems and security architect for AgFirst Farm Credit Bank where he worked on Active Directory, Windows security, VMware, and Citrix. In the technical community, Brian is president of the Midlands PASS Chapter, an official chapter of the Professional Association for SQL Server (PASS), as well as a regional mentor for the Mid-Atlantic chapters of PASS. Brian is also a junior high youth minister at Spears Creek Baptist Church in Elgin, SC.

www.ingramcontent.com/pod-product-compliance
Lightning Source LLC
Chambersburg PA
CBHW071159050326
40689CB00011B/2187